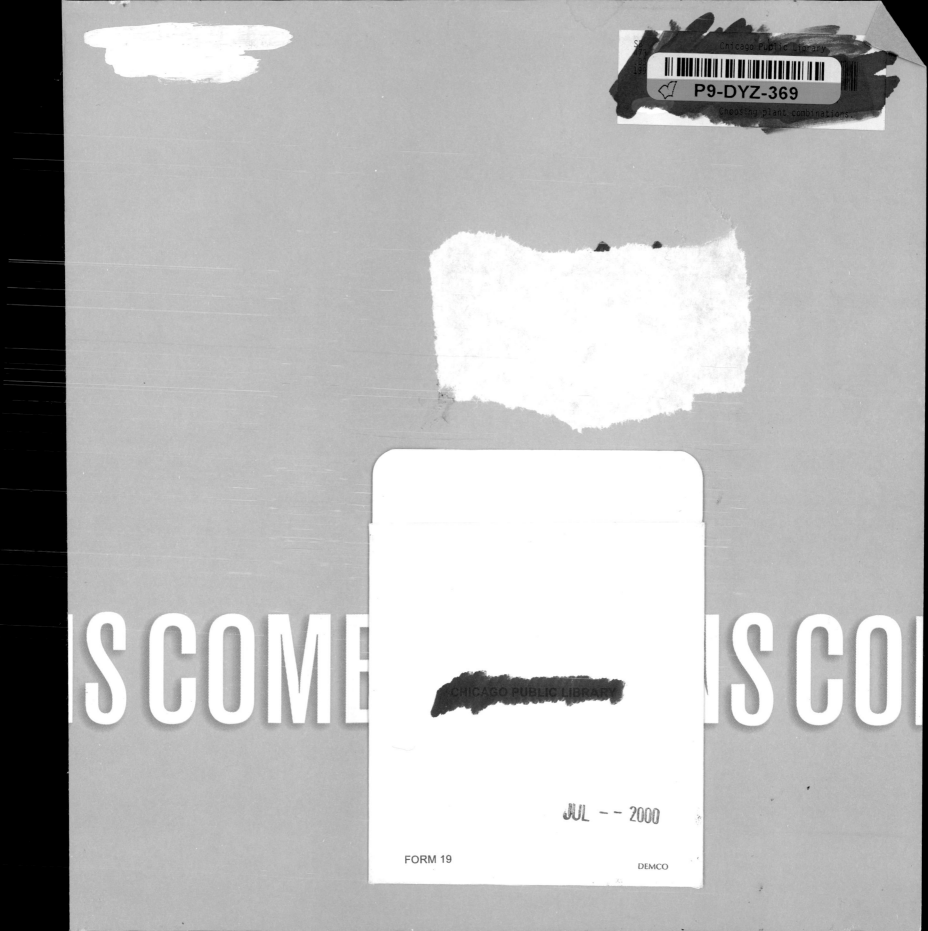

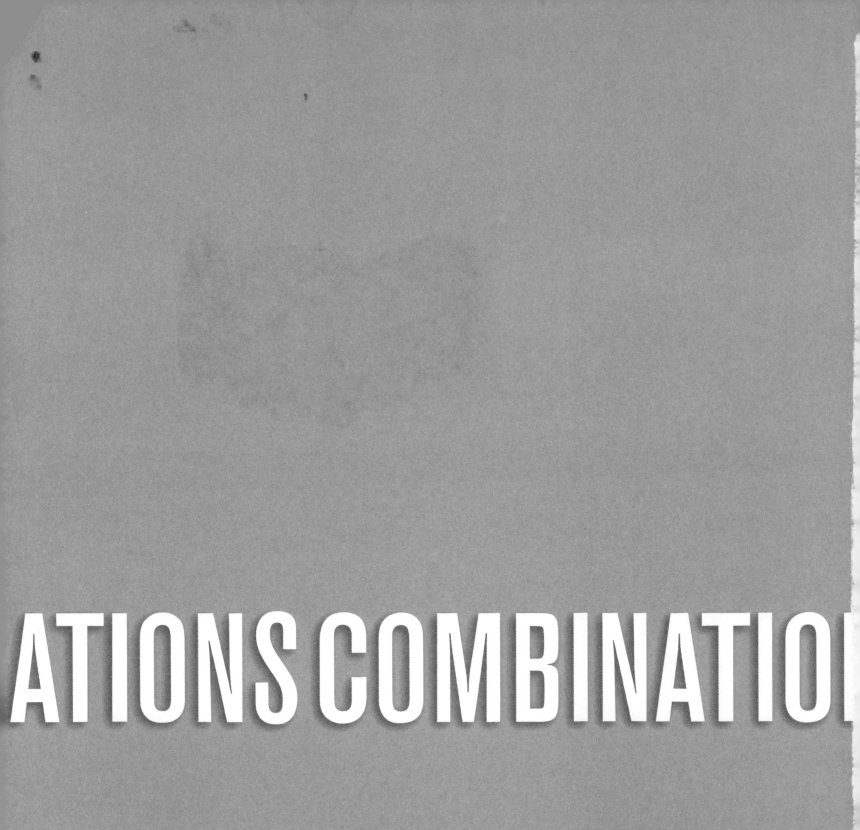

CHOOSING PLANT COMBINATIONS

BETTER HOMES AND GARDENS® BOOKS · DES MOINES, IOWA

BETTER HOMES AND GARDENS® BOOKS
AN IMPRINT OF MEREDITH® BOOKS

CHOOSING PLANT COMBINATIONS

Author: Cathy Wilkinson Barash

Senior Associate Design Director: Richard Michels

Contributing Editor: James A. Baggett

Copy Chief: Catherine Hamrick

Copy and Production Editor: Terri Fredrickson

Contributing Copy Editor: Jay Lamar

Contributing Proofreaders: Mary Duerson, Mary Pas, JoEllyn Witke

Contributing Photographer, Chapter Dividers: Howard Bjornson

Contributing Photographers: David Cavagnaro, Rosalind Creasy, R. Todd Davis, Joseph DeScoise, Dency Kane, Pete Krumhardt, Charles Mann, Carole Ottesen, Greg Ryan, Saba S. Tian

Photographs Courtesy of White Flower Farm: p. 140, p. 168 top right, p. 178 top right, p. 182 bottom

Indexer and Researcher: Leona Openshaw

Electronic Production Coordinator: Paula Forest

Editorial and Design Assistants: Kaye Chabot, Mary Lee Gavin, Karen Schirm

Production Director: Douglas M. Johnston

Production Manager: Pam Kvitne

Assistant Prepress Manager: Marjorie J. Schenkelberg

MEREDITH® BOOKS

Editor in Chief: James D. Blume

Design Director: Matt Strelecki

Managing Editor: Gregory H. Kayko

Director, Sales & Marketing, Retail: Michael A. Peterson

Director, Sales & Marketing, Special Markets: Rita McMullen

Director, Sales & Marketing, Home & Garden Center Channel: Ray Wolf

Director, Operations: George A. Susral

Vice President, General Manager: Jamie L. Martin

BETTER HOMES AND GARDENS® MAGAZINE

Editor in Chief: Jean LemMon

Executive Garden Editor: Mark Kane

MEREDITH PUBLISHING GROUP

President, Publishing Group: Christopher M. Little

Vice President, Consumer Marketing & Development: Hal Oringer

MEREDITH CORPORATION

Chairman and Chief Executive Officer: William T. Kerr

Chairman of the Executive Committee: E. T. Meredith III

All of us at Better Homes and Gardens® Books are dedicated to providing you with information and ideas to enhance your home and garden. We welcome your comments and suggestions. Write to us at: Better Homes and Gardens® Books, Garden Editorial Department, 1716 Locust St., Des Moines, IA 50309-3023. Or visit us at bhg.com

If you would like to purchase any of our books, check wherever quality books are sold.

Cover Photograph: Rosalind Creasy. The combination of Coreopsis 'Early Sunrise', Geranium 'Pinto Red', and Verbena 'Vervain' is shown on pages 98–99.

how to create a beautiful garden is

a matter of perspective—a simple but valuable idea that took root within me after years of photographing and writing about public and private gardens. When looking through my favorite 90-mm camera lens, I don't see the big picture. Instead, I focus on vignettes—combinations of two, three, four, or more plants. Each grouping grows as an individual aesthetic statement in addition to being a vital component of the overall scene. I began designing gardens that way—building on one combination after another. ■ Now that idea blooms on every page of *Choosing Plant Combinations*, which reveals the wonders of garden design, easily. In other words, this book shows you how color, shape, and texture work together in all sorts of plant groupings. Here's good garden design at your fingertips. So whether you're a novice or an experienced gardener, you now have the pleasure of planning, digging, planting, and taking in the fresh air, sights, and sounds of your garden without first sweating those intimidating rules about color and design. Enjoy your plant combinations as I do mine—as individual works of art and as parts of a larger, enchanting vision. —Cathy Wilkinson Barash

contents

COLOR COLOR COLOR COLOR COLOR COLO

single

subtle

bold

134

168

198

RM FORM FORM FORM FORM FORM FOR

single

subtle

bold

COMBINATION INTRODUCTION	COLOR INTRODUCTION	FORM INTRODUCTION	DESCRIPTION INDEX
6	16	128	236

Gardeners use their gardens as canvases, working with different flowers, foliage, and grasses to create living compositions that convey mood, style, and personality. Whether you're planting your first bed or trying a new look for your yard, *Choosing Plant Combinations* shows how you, too, can have an artist's flair in the garden. Simply use one or more of the plant combinations shown in this book as a basis for planting your garden. ■ It's fun to look through the pages of this book and see what your garden—or a part of the garden—can look like. *Choosing Plant Combinations* saves you the hassle, time, and money of going back and forth

intro

OMBINATIONS COMBIN

to the nursery, buying plants, setting them in the garden only to find after a year or more that they don't go well together. Then it's back to the nursery to try again. You'll never have to go through all that again—this book shows how the plants will look together when they're mature and in their peak of glory. ■ Gardening is a matter of perspective. Think one step at a time instead of looking at the big picture— even if you yearn for the 8-foot-deep and 50-foot-long double border. It's the combinations, vignettes, or small groupings—taken one at a time, and then grouped together—that make up a garden. With this book as a guide, you'll make definite plant choices rather than working by trial and error—putting plants in the garden that look good at the nursery, but not together in your garden. In short, we've done the research so you can easily picture, before selecting and planting, how the plants will bring new life to your yard. ■ It's easy to use

GARDEN WITH
BOLD-COLOR
COMBINATION

GARDEN WITH SUBTLE COLOR COMBINATION

Choosing Plant Combinations. Leaf leisurely through the book—nearly every page showcases wonderful garden combinations. Take note of the plant combinations that you like and are best suited to areas in your yard. You have plenty of choices, as this book includes plants common to the United States and Canada ■ Once you've selected the combinations you like, look up the plants in the descriptive index. At a glance, you can tell whether a plant is suitable for your garden. If your preferred plants won't grow in your hardiness zone, there are alternatives suggested for the plants in each combination that will give the same look, but extend the hardiness into a warmer or colder region. Make sure the light requirements, size, and height fit your garden. Write down the plant's name (common and botanical), and you have the all the information you need to go shopping. ■ You don't have to know anything about design to create a beautiful garden—*Choosing Plant Combinations* does

the work for you. Color and form are the two most important plant characteristics that professional garden designers and landscape architects take into account when creating a garden. For that reason, we've divided the combinations in the book into two main sections—color and form. And, each of those sections is further divided into single, subtle and bold. ■ Forget your grammar-school art teacher's pedantic explanation of the color wheel. Simply think about single, subtle, and bold colors. In a single-color plant combination, one color dominates. For instance, if you like red, choose a combination in which all the plants are the same shade or one that has varied shades. In the combination above (and on page 25) pink, red, and salmon-colored pinks gently mix with the carmine petals of cannas. Variations of sunny colors—brown-eyed Susans and French marigolds—nod happily on page 34. ■ A subtle color combination has a cool look, and generally consists of pale or pastel colors. Spring brings to mind these sweet combinations, such as pale purples and cheerful yellows of Virginia bluebells, daffodils, and woodland phlox (*below and on page 82*). Blues and greens reminiscent of a quiet sea make a calming background statement on page 72, with the appealing mix of Olympic mullein, larkspur, breadseed poppy, and rose campion. ■ Some gardens sizzle, almost explode, with bold colors. Hot and bright, these colors charge the senses. A dazzling display, like a modern work of art, demands attention on page 99, where coreopsis 'Early Sunrise', geranium 'Pinto Red', and verbena 'Vervain' make an incredible impression. ■ Of course, flowers aren't the sole source of plant color. Leaves, often overlooked for the flowers, come in almost every color of the rainbow, and multicolors, too. Each year there are more variegated plants on the market. Multihued, bold foliage plants, such as coleus and many tropical plants,

SUBTLE-COLOR COMBINATION

are all the rage (*below and page 115*). You may be familiar with many of them as houseplants, but they take on a new life when added to the summer garden outdoors. ■ If you live in an area with cold winters, seek out plants with colored stems and branches that will add life to the otherwise dull, barren, winter landscape. Shrubs

like variegated red-twig dogwood, whose colorful bark is hidden during the growing season by the leaves, provide magnificent color in an otherwise drab season. ■ The form section examines the overall plants as well as the leaves and flowers for shape, growth habit, size, and texture. This section, like the color section, is divided into three chapters—single, subtle, and bold combinations. With color, the differences between single, subtle, and bold are obvious. With form, however, a second glance is often necessary before you see similarities of shapes. ■ Single-form combinations include plants, flowers, or

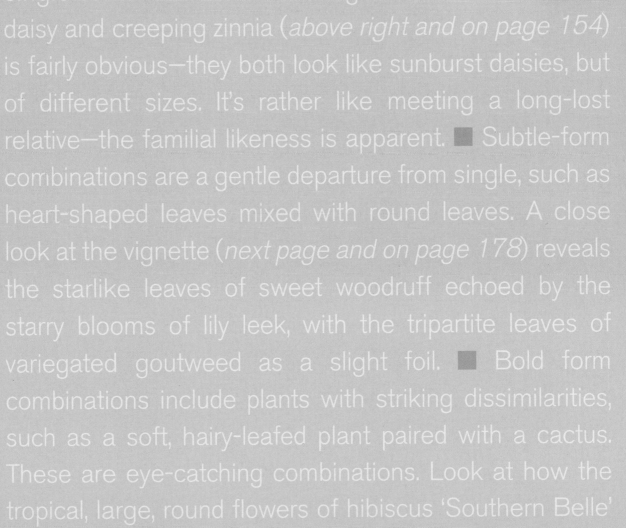

SINGLE-FORM
COMBINATION

leaves of the same shape, as well as
similarly textured plants. A plant with
round flowers may be paired with
another with round leaves, or with
another round-flowered plant. The
single-form combination of gloriosa
daisy and creeping zinnia (*above right and on page 154*)
is fairly obvious—they both look like sunburst daisies, but
of different sizes. It's rather like meeting a long-lost
relative—the familial likeness is apparent. ■ Subtle-form
combinations are a gentle departure from single, such as
heart-shaped leaves mixed with round leaves. A close
look at the vignette (*next page and on page 178*) reveals
the starlike leaves of sweet woodruff echoed by the
starry blooms of lily leek, with the tripartite leaves of
variegated goutweed as a slight foil. ■ Bold form
combinations include plants with striking dissimilarities,
such as a soft, hairy-leafed plant paired with a cactus.
These are eye-catching combinations. Look at how the
tropical, large, round flowers of hibiscus 'Southern Belle'

glow against the airy blooms of hydrangea 'Tardiva' (*page 200*). ■ Although this book presents color and form in separate sections for purposes of basic explanation, you need to consider both when sizing up a plant grouping. A fine example of both bold color and form (*next page and on page 201*) has sculpted red petals of montbretia complementing the seed heads of Russian globe thistle. ■ Approach selecting plant combinations as you would choosing new furniture for a room. Do you focus only on the shape of chairs and sofas without giving a thought to the colors or textures of upholstery? As you look at all the options, your mind will open to more planting possibilities than you ever imagined. The bottom line is personal preference. All that matters is that you like the combination, whether it's bold, subtle, or single. ■ When you have the list of plants that will work in your garden in hand, you're ready to go shopping. There are more good sources for plants—both locally and nationally—than you might have imagined. Numerous nurseries, large and small, and home and garden centers have a wide choice of plant material. You may also want to explore passalong plants from friends, neighbors, and relatives. Look in their gardens for the plants you're seeking. Often, in return for helping divide plants in spring or fall, they'll give you divisions of a large plant from their garden. Other sources of inexpensive plants— properly named and well cared for— are plant sales at local gardens or schools. If you can't find a plant at a local nursery, home center, or garden shop, investigate the mail-order and

BOLD-FORM COMBINATION

online sources at the back of the book. ■ At last it's time to plant the garden. Most plants benefit from compost or other organic matter mixed into the soil at planting time. Once in the ground, give them all a drink of water and keep the plants well-watered until they're established. Then sit back and watch the garden grow and bloom.

COLOR COLOR COLOR C

LOR COLOR COLOR CO

Color makes the first—and lasting—impression on anyone looking at a garden. Whether the color choices in the garden reflect a monochromatic color scheme, a mixture of subtle colors, or a palette of bold colors, the colors strongly influence the overall experience of that garden. ■ Simply by adding different colored plants to an existing garden, the mood is radically changed. Take a partially shaded area under some evergreen and deciduous trees, for example. Plant a combination of ferns and foliage plants, such as wild and European ginger, and mayapple. The result is a cool-looking, single-color (green) scene that's very natural and serene. Now add some hostas—some of the blue-leafed forms and a few white-variegated ones. The addition of these plants and their muted colors brightens the dark corners, creating a subtle color combination. Jazz it up with some brightly colored azaleas and several yellow or chartreuse-variegated hostas and it turns into a bold combination. There's a place for every type of combination—it's all a matter of personal taste. Cultivate *your* favorite colors. ■ Even though the flowers (or leaves) in a single-color combination are the same color, such a grouping isn't boring or bland. An all-white garden, such as the famed garden of Vita-Sackville West at Sissinghurst, is very serene. However, the effect of a single color garden may not always be so calming. Some gardeners are cultivating black-flowered gardens, which are quite somber affairs. How about a pink garden? The effect depends on the pinks used. Compare the reaction to pastel pink flowers with that of bright fuchsia pink blooms. Pink—like all other colors—runs the gamut from calm and cooling to brash and hot as the color intensifies from pale pastel to fully saturated. ■ The flower colors need not match one another exactly. In fact, it's more interesting to have different hues or shades of the same color together. The entire garden, however, need not be a single color, even when working with single-color combinations. Consider a rainbow garden, using all the single-color combinations to create a rainbow effect. This is best done with annuals

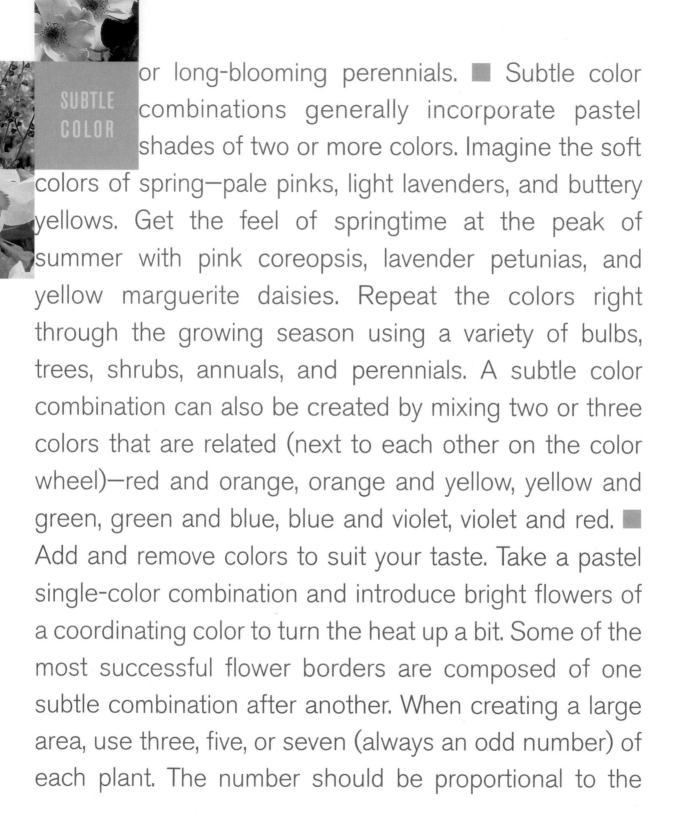

or long-blooming perennials. ■ Subtle color combinations generally incorporate pastel shades of two or more colors. Imagine the soft colors of spring—pale pinks, light lavenders, and buttery yellows. Get the feel of springtime at the peak of summer with pink coreopsis, lavender petunias, and yellow marguerite daisies. Repeat the colors right through the growing season using a variety of bulbs, trees, shrubs, annuals, and perennials. A subtle color combination can also be created by mixing two or three colors that are related (next to each other on the color wheel)—red and orange, orange and yellow, yellow and green, green and blue, blue and violet, violet and red. ■ Add and remove colors to suit your taste. Take a pastel single-color combination and introduce bright flowers of a coordinating color to turn the heat up a bit. Some of the most successful flower borders are composed of one subtle combination after another. When creating a large area, use three, five, or seven (always an odd number) of each plant. The number should be proportional to the size of each plant—bigger for small plants, and smaller for large perennials or shrubs. Otherwise, the resulting garden would be a hodgepodge. ■ Bold combinations are eye-catching melanges of bright colors. Often the mix is simply bright primary (red, yellow, and blue) or secondary (orange, green, and violet) colors. Purple and chartreuse, and other variations of the complementary colors are other bold combos. Such vivid combinations are still new and exciting—mixes that no one did 20 years ago—and they're popping up everywhere. ■ Use the bold colors in the garden to laugh at the weather or the time of year. In regions with cool summers or frequent rain showers, choose from the bold color combinations to heat up and brighten the garden. Imagine starting spring with bright yellow crocuses, red tulips, and orange hyacinths. ■ Working with bold colors tends to bring out the creative child in many gardeners. And if playing with color in the garden is like painting a picture, using bold colors in profusion is like finger painting—what fun!

BOLD COLOR

Single-color combinations are beautiful in their simplicity. Start by choosing one plant with an appealing color—remember that leaves can play into the color scheme, too. Once you've picked a color, you're open to the infinite variations of that color for the other plants. Match the color exactly or go for its lighter and darker shades. Finding an exact match can be more challenging than it might seem—flower colors vary depending on the amount of sun or shade they get. When looking for a match, it's better to shop locally, choosing plants that are already in bloom. Depending on the color chosen, the combination may be bright and intense or pale and soothing.

single

The juxtaposition of closely related plants that share similar coloration is an excellent way to create pairings that resonate. Continuity is provided by similarity in color and habit. Plants: *from top:* Amaranth 'Illumination', Amaranth 'Joseph's Coat'. Alternatives: Coleus 'Gay's Delight', Coleus 'Wine and Lime'.

reiterate color from related plants

celebrate
with crimson

Crank up the intensity of color in the

garden with unabashed crimson

colors. Raise the level of interest with an

elevated tier of reflected red

blooms. Plants: *from top:* Canna 'President',

Zinnia 'State Fair Mix'.

Alternatives: Lobelia 'Bee's Flame',

Caladium 'Cardinal'.

unify by repeating colors

Look for sources of color repetition besides

flowers. Consider the color of leaves,

stems, bark, and berries, as well as seasonal

color changes. Plants: *clockwise from*

top left: Shrimp Plant, Cleistocactus, Aloe,

Rockspray Cotoneaster. Alternatives:

Pyracantha 'Navajo', Great Burnet, Yucca,

New Guinea Impatiens 'Macarena'.

bold choices with coleus

Mix and match loudly variegated plants for kaleidoscopic color effects repeated in different leaf patterns. For widest selection and consistency, buy named varieties grown from cuttings. Plants: Coleus 'Wizard Mix' (grown from seed). Alternatives: Coleus 'Antique', 'Eclipse', 'Flair', 'Mardi Gras'.

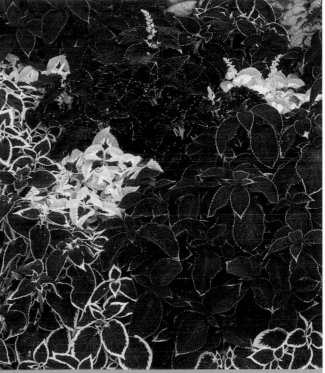

razzle-dazzle reds

Red is one of the most versatile hues in the garden. Choose similar shades in various shapes. Plants: *clockwise from top left:* Salvia 'Lady in Red', Zinnia 'Scarlet Splendor', Scarlet Sage 'Empire Purple'. Alternatives: Astilbe 'Red Sentinel', Bee Balm 'Gardenview Scarlet', Verbena 'Taylortown Red'.

27

Instead of trying to match

shades of color exactly, use a darker or lighter shade

of the same color for the backdrop

plants. Plants: *from top:* Cactus Dahlias, Sedum

'Autumn Joy'. Alternatives: Rose

'Abraham Darby', Garden Phlox 'Orange Perfection'.

create drama with varied hues

find variety in variegation

Variegation—leaves that are marked, striped, or blotched with a color (usually white or cream) other than green—adds interest to humdrum situations and enlivens dreary corners. Plants: *from top left:* Dracaena 'Tricolor', Copperleaf, Lantana. Alternatives: Twisted-Leaf Yucca, Chameleon Plant, Cranesbill.

shades of orange

Oranges provide an excellent balance between ruby-to-mahogany reds and similarly intense yellows. Allow the lighter or darker hues to serve as a backdrop and show off the purest shades. Plants: *from top:* Cactus Dahlia, Montbretia. Alternatives: Lily 'Enchantment', Verbena 'Peaches & Cream'.

vary the shape but stick with the color

When working within a single-color palette,

create interest by mixing

flower sizes and shapes—round and tubular,

trumpet-shaped and daisylike. Take

a look at plant catalogs for ideas. Plants:

from top left: Masterwort, Cape

Fuchsia. Alternatives: Nasturtium 'Apricot

Twist', Salvia 'Cherry Blossom'.

go for the golds

When maintaining the tight color palette of a single-color vignette, shape and texture become important considerations. Combine flowers of contrasting habits for heightened interest. Plants: *from left:* Golden Carpet, Yarrow 'Moonshine'. Alternatives: Lady's Mantle 'Thriller', *Aurinia corymbosa.*

draw sunny circles

Combinations of similarly shaped flowers benefit from points of differentiations such as dramatic centers or variations in petal coloration or shape. Plants: *clockwise from top left:* Gloriosa Daisy, Coreopsis 'Early Sunrise', Blanket Flower 'Dazzler'. Alternatives: Sunflower, Lance Coreopsis, Gloriosa Daisy 'Goldilocks'.

serve fruit with flowers

For those fortunate enough to live in warm climates that support citrus trees, consider allowing a nonaggressive flowering vine to clamber up the trunk to decorate the fruited boughs year-round. Plants: *from top left:* Calamondin Tree, *Senecio scandens.* Alternatives: Meyer Lemon, Canary Creeper.

beware of beautiful invaders

Some appealing plants in nurseries and garden centers are thugs. Left unchecked in the garden, they are rampant spreaders that may suffocate less strident and more delicate neighbors in time. Plants: *from top:* Daffodil 'Actaea', Lesser Celandine. Alternatives: Daffodil 'Flower Record', Basket-of-Gold.

spice it up with annual seed mixes

Many annuals, such as marigolds, nasturtiums, and

zinnias, are available in packets of seed

mixes that feature a range of shades of a single color—or a

spectrum of rainbow flowers. Plants: *from top:*

Brown-Eyed Susan, French Marigold. Alternatives:

Melampodium, Zinnia 'Whirligig Mix'.

radiate light and movement

Golden summer yellows hold on to their color in brilliant light, partial shade, on gray days, even in the rain. Contrasting blossom shapes and tonal variations make for winning combinations. Plants: *from top left:* False Sunflower 'Ballerina', Daylily 'Hyperion'. Alternatives: Lily 'Connecticut King', Perennial Sunflower.

play up the
subtleties

A quick glance at this combination shows

plants of two different colors. Yet a

closer look reveals that the iris buds echo

the foxglove's color. And when the

iris opens, its deep yellow throat offers

lively interest. Plants: *from left:*

Yellow Foxglove, Spuria Iris. Alternatives:

Baby's Breath 'Gypsy', Celosia 'Amazon'.

chartreuse, if you please

All kinds of plants boast this glowing pistachio color. After all, spring is full of it. Pot up plants of this cheerful color to place as accents where needed. They are especially suited for lighting up shady corners. Plants: *from left:* Hakone Grass, Hosta 'Sun Power'. Alternatives: Japanese Sweet Flag, Coleus 'Limeline'.

Although many plants have chartreuse leaves, others are variegated green and gold, and only give the impression of this lighthearted color. Variegated choices consort well with yellow plants. Plants: *from top:* Bowles Golden Grass, Common Sage 'Icterina'. Alternatives: Yellow Foxtail Grass, Variegated Winter Creeper.

create the illusion of chartreuse

illuminate
the landscape

A look at the colors of variegation in garden

plants shows that nature doesn't

observe any formulas. It uses chartreuse

with confidence and abandon, as

should home gardeners. Plants: *from left:*

Yucca 'Gold Sword', Coleus 'Pineapple

Queen'. Alternatives: New Zealand Flax

'Radiance', Tovara 'Painter's Palette'.

discover night fragrance

Some flowers are fragrant only at night. Others, like hosta,

have a stronger scent in the evening. Put one

in your garden and you'll be amazed to see the pollinators,

such as luna moths, that visit. Plants: *from top:*

Hosta montana, Astilbe 'White Gloria'. Alternatives:

Flowering Tobacco, Ground Clematis.

Take time to enjoy the garden when white flowers glow in the moonlight. Plants: *from top:* Poppy Anemone 'De Caen Hybrids', Petunia, Sweet Alyssum, Nemesia 'White Innocence'. Alternatives: Vinca 'Mediterranean White', Pansy 'Giant White', Cupflower 'Mont Blanc', Edging Lobelia 'Paper Moon'.

see luminescent white at night

cultivate nighttime magic

At night, dark colors—including green— disappear in the gloom. A garden takes on a magical quality when all you see are the white outlines of variegated leaves or white blooms that seem to float on air. Plants: *from top left:* Hosta 'Northern Halo', Lily-of-the-Valley. Alternatives: Variegated Goutweed, Shooting Star.

let whites light the night

Shrubs with white flowers or white berries

lend the garden height

and luster when combined with perennials

boasting white flowers or

variegation. Plants: *from top:* Smooth

Hydrangea, *Hosta crispula.*

Alternatives: Burkwood Viburnum, Japanese

Euonymus 'Silver Knight'.

go green on
green

Note the subtle differences in leaf color

of groundcovers, including the

shape, texture, and habit. Large, shiny leaves

contrast nicely with fine

whorled foliage, inviting closer inspection.

Plants: *from top:* Sweet Woodruff,

European Ginger. Alternatives: Cliff-

Green, London Pride.

make SIZE matter

The beauty of combining intriguing foliage is in echoing the leaf size and shape. Match the coloration or variegation of the foliage but in vastly different sizes. Plants: *from top:* Japanese Wavy-Leaved Hosta, Variegated Goutweed. Alternatives: Variegated Pachysandra, Silver and Gold.

look at the leaves

Many perennial flowers are fleeting—it's the foliage that's visible most of the season. Make the most of variegation, textures, and shapes. Plants: *clockwise from top left:* Japanese Painted Fern, Japanese Anemone, Spotted Lungwort. Alternatives: English Ivy 'Baltica', Foamflower, Japanese Wild Ginger.

take foliage to new heights

Start with a familiar solid-green groundcover such as ivy. Then dig in a bolder, more textural plant that will rise up a foot or more. The green base of the groundcover is much more interesting than mulch. Plants: *from left:* English Ivy, Bear's Breeches. Alternatives: Periwinkle, Stinking Hellebore.

light colorful fireworks

Anchor spectacular clusters of blue flowers to the surrounding landscape with a low-growing groundcover capable of producing simpler blossoms in a similar shade. Plants: *from top:* Star-of-Persia, Geranium 'Johnson's Blue'. Alternatives: *Allium karataviense,* Creeping Phlox 'Blue Ridge'.

Silver and silver-blue foliage plants add a cool touch of elegance to beds and borders alike. Ironically, they're usually tough plants that can take the heat—they're drought-tolerant and enjoy full sun. Plants: *from top:* Wormwood, Cuban Oregano. Alternatives: Lavender Cotton, Pussytoes.

the cool elegance of silvery foliage

add diversity
with bicolored blooms

When exploring a monochromatic theme,

add a plant with bicolored flowers,

preferably including a pristine white.

Plants: *from top:* Lupine 'The

Governor', Geranium 'Johnson's Blue', Salvia

'May Night'. Alternatives: Delphinium

'Connecticut Yankee', Carpathian Harebell,

Rocky Mountain Columbine.

let the blues take the stage

The best blues can play a solid, if not a starring, role in summer situations. Blues can be difficult to match, so sit back and appreciate the wealth of choices in the color palette. Plants *from top:* Geranium 'Johnson's Blue', Catmint. Alternatives: Ceratostigma, Monkshood 'Bressingham Spire'.

A few perennials are rich in blues; some have silvery blue leaves. Use flowers to bring out the color in foliage growing nearby. Plants: *clockwise from top:* Salvia 'Blue Bedder', Lungwort, Artemisia 'Powis Castle'. Alternatives: Spiderwort 'Zwanenburg Blue', Hosta 'Elegans', Beach Wormwood.

the blues are cool

play with polka dots

Take a lighthearted approach to gardening. Pair plants with pink polka dots or variegation with pompons of blushing blooms to bring smiles to visitors' faces.

Plants: *from top:* Impatiens 'Fiesta Pink', Polka-Dot Plant 'Splash Select Pink'. Alternatives: Canterbury Bells 'Russian Pink', Caladium 'Little Miss Muffet'.

open up the range of color

Take a step beyond single-colored flowers.

Add bicolored plants for a cool

look to the garden. Go the full range of a

color—here, from the palest

pink through rosy pink to lavender. Plants:

from front: Bearded Iris, Peony

'Sarah Bernhardt'. Alternatives: Snow

Crocus, Lenten Rose.

51

centers of attention

Flowers with accentuated centers add an element of surprise. Such cheerful accents include blossoms sporting round eyes and deeply veined throats. For an exciting mix, pair two with contrasting centers. Plants: *from top*: Petunia, Maiden Pinks. Alternatives: Gladiola 'Pallas', Lavatera 'Eye Catcher'.

dare to be different

Many gardens have the same old plants. Be adventurous and explore the garden catalogs. Grow plants suited to your climate that you've never grown before. Plants: *from top:* Veined Verbena, Tufted Evening Primrose, Prickly Pear Cactus. Alternatives: Dwarf Creeping Indigo, Rock Rose, Hens-and-Chicks.

create
echoes
of color

Repetition of color catches the eye and soothes the soul. Consider the ornamental value of edibles and mimic shape and texture for stunning results. Plants: *from top:* Chrysanthemum, Ornamental Kale. Alternatives: Hollyhock 'The Watchman Strain', Purple Brussels Sprouts.

let colors
clamber

Allow plants with striking foliage to wander through a mass of flowers to create their own idiosyncratic design. Consider letting two climbers intermingle at ground level. Plants: *from top:* Violet-Flowered Petunia, Tradescantia 'Purple Heart'. Alternatives: Morning Glory 'Chocolate', New Zealand Flax 'Burgundy'.

don't be afraid of the dark

Tender and tropical plants have a great range of colors. Accent the darkest color in a multihued leaf with a dark-colored flower. Dark foliage is unexpected, adding a sense of mystery. Plants: *from top:* Coleus 'Rob Roy', Tradescantia 'Purple Heart'. Alternatives: Caladium 'Sweetheart', Black Mondo Grass.

Small bedding plants can be especially effective when they're paired with deep-hued flowers of a more static, architectural nature as a backdrop. Blossoms with interesting details offer additional diversity. Plants: *from top:* Purple Beardtongue, Cottage Pinks. Alternatives: *Campanula garganica,* Mazus.

pay attention to the details

toss edible flowers together

Dual-purpose flowering plants save garden

space, whether they are for

cutting or cooking. Grow edible flowers

organically—from seeds or

transplants—as an added bonus for your

dinner table. Plants: *from top left:*

Chives, Rose 'La Belle Sultane'. Alternatives:

English Daisy, Tulip 'Baronesse'.

It's fun to pair plants that are somewhat similar

in flower shape. Select plants with related

colors and allow foliage to serve as a distinguishing

characteristic for confused guests.

Plants: *from top left:* Cranesbill, Dianthus. Alternatives:

Aster × frikartii, Cineraria.

reveal the identity of similar plants

Subtle color combinations conjure up visions of English cottage gardens with voluptuous flowers in subdued colors—mostly pale pink, muted blue, light purple, and white, perhaps with a dash of pale lemon yellow. They include many traditional pairings—pink and blue, yellow and silver, blue and white, yellow and white—in well-modulated tones. A garden made entirely of subtle combinations doesn't have the attention-grabbing brilliance of a bold garden. Instead, it's like an old, trusted friend—comfortable and familiar, with no surprises. If you prefer, enliven it a bit with one brightly or contrastingly colored flower. Or just sit back and enjoy its beauty.

subtle

LOR COLOR COLOR CO

frolic with shades of pink and white

Fuchsia creates a magnificent accent when

combined with white and not-so-

intense shades of blush. Plants: *clockwise from top center:*

Cheddar Pinks, Snow-in-Summer, Cottage

Pinks, Common Sage. Alternatives: Creeping Phlox,

Candytuft, Moss Pinks, Blue-Eyed Mary.

Choose yellows with care. Cool-toned yellows create a softer color contrast than their lemon yellow counterparts. Plants: *clockwise from top left:* Jupiter's Beard, Verbascum 'Southern Charm', Bloody Cranesbill 'Album'. Alternatives: Phlox 'Phlox of Sheep', Snapdragon 'Jamaican Mist', Cupflower 'Mont Blanc'.

make a romantic scene

color sets the mood

Cool blues can increase a garden's

spaciousness and mystery. Pale

pink enhances its tranquil effect. Plants:

from left: Geranium 'Wargrave

Pink', English Lavender, Variegated Purple

Moor Grass. Alternatives: Showy

Evening Primrose 'Pink Petticoats', Catmint,

Variegated Japanese Sedge.

work in some cooling colors

In the heat of summer, pale pink and white are cooling colors to border a walkway or garden bed. They reflect the moonlight, so they're perfect in an evening garden. Plants: *from top:* Flowering Tobacco 'Domino Salmon Pink', Petunia 'White Magic'. Alternatives: Hollyhock Mallow, Datura 'Alba'.

Gardeners often ignore vines and climbers. These plants can add another dimension by drawing the eye upward. Use them to hide less attractive vertical features such as walls or fences. Plants: *from top left:* Lady Banks Rose, Anemone Clematis. Alternatives: Chilean Jasmine, Carolina Jessamine.

add a vertical element

shine a ray of light

Shades of dark purple benefit from a shot of pink to enliven a mass of plants, like a beam of light shining directly at the front of the border. Tip: These are all good cut flowers. Plants: from left: Siberian Catmint, Gladiola 'Violetta', Rose 'Sparrieshoop'. Alternatives: Camas, Triplet Lily, Tulip 'Renown'.

weave a tapestry of color

Pale peach petals intermingle with a cloud

of blue in the background to form a

lovely late-summer combination. These

restrained hues are a portent of

deeper shades to come. Plants: *from left:*

Bluebeard, Russian Hollyhock.

Alternatives: Blue False Indigo, Golden

Columbine 'Silver Queen'.

explore
different visual
effects from foliage

Variegated plants have never been more

popular. Brighten shady spaces

with the addition of various leaves dappled

with illuminating creams, whites,

and silvers. Plants: *from top:* Japanese

Painted Fern, Lungwort 'Mrs.

Moon'. Alternatives: Lilyturf 'John Burch',

Spotted Dead Nettle.

soften it with filigreed
silver

The handsome froth of silvery foliage

makes a lovely foil for an essential

palette of pink and silver, with a note of

deep purple. Plants: *clockwise from top*

left: Wormwood 'Lambrook Silver', Star

Cluster, Purple Perilla. Alternatives:

Dusty Miller 'Silver Dust', Rose-Scented

Geranium, Basil 'Purple Ruffles'.

jazz it up with purple leaves

Introduce a dark-leafed plant among

variegated leaves and the combination

takes on a different character from the

one above. Plants: *clockwise from left:*

Variegated Licorice Plant, Variegated

Society Garlic, Knotweed 'Magic Carpet'.

Alternatives: Lamb's Ears, Variegated

Bulbous Oat Grass, Purple Oxalis.

pull a quick
change with color

Many plants produce buds of a lighter

or darker shade than the actual

flower color. It's fascinating to watch the

depth and dimension they add to

the garden as they seductively unfurl their

petals. Plants: *from top:* Fringed

Bleeding Heart, Spanish Bluebells.

Alternatives: Astilbe, Culver's Root 'Roseum'.

A dominant, cool-hued, silvery green background plant will tone down warmer foreground colors. Select plants to create a tapestry of textures. Plants: *from top:* Sedum 'Moonglow', Threadleaf Coreopsis 'Moonbeam', New England Aster. Alternatives: Boltonia, Daylily 'Stella d'Oro', Garden Phlox 'Blue Paradise'.

tone it down with cool colors

let plants
commingle

Allow wiry-stemmed plants and nonaggressive

vines to interweave with

neighboring shrubs or perennials. This is an

easy way to create subtle bursts of

color that appear to be floating on air. Plants:

from top left: Freeway Daisy,

California Poppy. Alternatives: Dahlia 'Pretty

in Pink', Yellow Climbing Lily.

Good color transitions come from careful

selection and placement of foliage

and flowering plants. Plants: *clockwise from

top left:* Prince's Feather 'Golden

Giant', Dahlia 'Burma Gem', Coleus 'Alabama

Sunset', Golden Japanese Barberry.

Alternatives: Yellow Meadow Rue, Knautia,

Tovara 'Painter's Palette', Yellow Moneywort.

delve
into wine-colored foliage

Dark colors supply contrast and opposite colors create harmonious scenes when luminous flowers are combined with deep burgundy foliage plants. Plants: *from top left:* Threadleaf Coreopsis 'Zagreb', Sedum 'Honey Song'. Alternatives: Ligularia 'The Rocket', Sea Holly 'Blue Ribbon'.

Sedums give foliage interest for much of the year, and they're showstoppers when they bloom. Here they are used to echo the grass color. Plants: *clockwise from top left:* Japanese Bloodgrass, Ground Clematis, Sedum 'Rosy Glow'. Alternatives: New Zealand Flax, Dwarf Baby's Breath, Bugleweed.

fall color repetition

feel the **soothing** effects of blue

Background colors, such as blues and greens, naturally reinforce one another and unify a saturated palette. Plants: *from top left:* Olympic Mullein, Larkspur, Breadseed Poppy, Rose Campion. Alternatives: Eryngium 'Miss Wilmott's Ghost', *Salvia viridis, Allium karataviense,* Clary Sage.

enjoy the ever-changing show

Gardens that flow seamlessly from season to season include plants that bloom at different times staggered around the garden. Plants: *clockwise from top left:* Delphinium 'Blue Springs', Fleabane 'Azure Fairy', Artemisia 'Silver King'. Alternatives: Texas Bluebonnet, Bee Balm 'Aquarius', Blue Fescue.

use large plant groupings

Drifts or swaths of plants lend an air of spaciousness, with breathing room among patches of seasonal color. Plants: *clockwise from top left:* Blue Salvia 'Victoria', False Sunflower 'Summer Sun', Catmint, Sweet Alyssum 'Carpet of Snow'. Alternatives: Larkspur, Melampodium, Majoricum, Snow-in-Summer.

tame
plants of the prairie

The airy feeling of this combination is

reminiscent of a natural meadow.

Yet it would work in a small urban yard,

creating the illusion of country.

Plants: *from left:* Wild Chicory, Common

Fleabane, Gloriosa Daisy.

Alternatives: Love-in-a-Mist, Baby's Breath,

St. John's Chamomile.

go for pale-toned
harmonies

Harmonies of light shades, even those of

contrasting colors, can soften the

overall effect of a bed or border. Conversely,

deep shades can intensify the

effect of the planting. Plants: *from top:*

Marguerite Daisy 'Jamaica

Primrose', Mist Flower. Alternatives:

Ageratum, Prickly Poppy.

cozy up to wooly leaves

Wooly or silver-leafed plants are

ideal to combine with

brazen-colored blossoms. Citrus yellow

blooms add a burst of

sunlight against a gray sky. Plants:

from top left: Lamb's Ears,

Lily Leek. Alternatives: Dollar Cactus,

Acacia 'Prostrata'.

feast
on spring edibles

Never underestimate the ability of an

edible—flower or leaf—to delight

the eye as well as the palate. Young spring

salad greens double as handsome

ornamentals. Plants: *clockwise from top left:*

Cabbage 'Early Jersey Wakefield',

Pansy, Lettuce 'Brunia'. Alternatives: Bok

Choy, Sweet Violet, Red Orach.

cool | the excitement

Muffle the effects of neon-bright
vermilion with a foreground planting
of a cool-colored blossom that is
within the same color family. Narrow,
straplike leaves provide an added
element of interest. Plants: *from top:*
Rose Campion, Spiderwort. Alternatives:
Japanese Primrose, Pasqueflower.

clear and crisp, blue and white

Blue and white is a favorite garden color scheme repeated in nature. In pure shades, the combination can be simply breathtaking (and is refreshing on hot summer days). Plants: *from left:* Japanese Iris 'Henry's White', Delphinium 'Blue Springs'. Alternatives: Musk Mallow 'Alba', Veronica 'Crater Lake Blue'.

point the way with grasses

Ornamental grasses are an important part of a foliage mix, creating carefree patterns throughout the seasons. Plants: *clockwise from top:* Ribbon Grass, Meadow Foxtail, Dwarf Blue Fescue, Penstemon 'Husker Red'. Alternatives: Manna Grass, Hakone Grass, Blue Lyme Grass, New Zealand Flax 'Burgundy'.

pink perks
up beautifully

Pink is dramatically affected by other colors. When placed next to deep burgundy red, its pale hue makes a striking statement. A background of green foliage makes pinks appear redder. Plants: *from top:* Purpleleaf Sand Cherry, Rose 'Betty Prior'. Alternatives: Purple Smokebush, Sheep Laurel 'Rubra'.

Deep purple flatters masses of soft pink and ivory. Contrasts of light and dark shades are invaluable for simplifying a color scheme. Plants: *from top:* Zinnia 'Ivory', Geranium 'Pink Elite', Scarlet Sage 'Laser Purple'. Alternatives: Marigold 'Vanilla Cream', Cosmos, Broadleafed Penstemon.

fine tune colors for
exquisite results

Meadow gardens attract birds, bees and butterflies by the score. Be sure to create a vantage point to view the vista. Plants: *clockwise from top left:* Garden Phlox, Swamp Sunflower, Garlic Chives, Purple Coneflower. Alternatives: Jupiter's Beard, Sulfur Cinquefoil, Plantain Thrift, Checkerbloom.

make a habitat for wildlife

celebrate spring's
soft colors

Beginning in spring, pale purples and yellows—so complementary—make for beautiful garden scenes. Plants: *clockwise from top left:* Virginia Bluebell, Daffodils, Woodland Phlox, Cypress Spurge, Violet. Alternatives: Lungwort, Tulip 'Mrs. John T. Scheepers', Siberian Bugloss, Lady's Mantle, Periwinkle.

go wild in the woodlands

Plant wildflowers under deciduous trees that provide dappled sunlight throughout the day. Since the plants don't require cultivation, the tree's roots won't be disturbed. Plants: *clockwise from left,* Western Mugwort, Oxeye Daisy, Bergamot. Alternatives: Russian Sage, Nippon Chrysanthemum, Stokes' Aster.

echo the pale flower tones

Tall, stately flower spikes in fiery colors become less intense when they are provided with warm, soothing pastel colors as the backdrop. Plants: *from front:* Red Hot Poker, Rose 'Brandy', Love-in-a-Mist 'Miss Jekyll Hybrid'. Alternatives: Foxtail Lily, Marigold 'Vanilla Cream', Pincushion Flower 'Pink Mist'.

single out one flower

The eye is drawn to the largest flower, then to those closest to

it; in the foreground it highlights other plants.

Plants: *clockwise from top left:* Coneflower 'Herbstonne', Tall

Verbena, Balloon Flower 'Komachi', Hibiscus

'Disco Belle Hybrids'. Alternatives: Elecampane, Mist Flower,

Ladybells, Showy Evening Primrose.

build visual textures with flowers

Delicate blue blossoms look striking

growing up through a mass of

soft, fluffy pink flowers. Encourage plants to

cavort with each other as long

as they don't compete for resources. Plants:

from front: True Forget-Me-Not,

Astilbe 'Peach Blossom'. Alternatives:

Chaste Tree, Tamarisk.

punctuate with a splash of color

Add a harmonious pastel accent to beckon

visitors beyond the garden gate. A

white picket fence with flowers billowing

through the pickets lends a country

attitude. Plants: *from front:* Jupiter's Beard,

Delphinium 'Pacific Giant Hybrids'.

Alternatives: Garden Phlox 'Bright Eyes',

Lupine 'Russell Hybrids'.

maintain a tight palette

The range of hues from dark to light within any one color is almost limitless. Pair the darker hues with the lighter ones for an interesting twist on a monochromatic combination. Plants *from top left:* Jupiter's Beard, Marguerite Daisy 'Vancouver'. Alternatives: Stock 'Appleblossom', Dianthus 'Ipswich Pinks'.

You can't go wrong when planting spring bulbs. Any of the pastel-hued ones go well together. Plant them in large drifts, not in soldierly rows. Plants: *from top left:* Tulip 'Grand Style', Hyacinth 'Pink Perfection', Grape Hyacinth. Alternatives: Yellow Crown Imperial, Tulip 'Angelique', Spanish Bluebells.

let the color drift on

The first two chapters on color—single and subtle—got you started experimenting with color in the garden. Soon, you'll want to do more and really express yourself with color. Unlike in the past decades when soft pastel gardens were de rigueur and monochromatic schemes were fashionable, today's gardeners are having fun playing with intense, bright colors—fuchsia pink, lemon yellow, chartreuse, cherry red, eggplant purple, pumpkin orange, and others. Primary colors are in. If it starts getting too hot for your taste, add a silver-leafed or white-flowered plant to cool down the sizzle. Remember, it's your garden, and you're the only one who has to like it.

bold

embrace primary colors

Flamboyant flowers add pizazz throughout the growing season. Those with large blossoms make the strongest impact. This brilliant combination carries the garden from summer into autumn. Plants: *from top:* Montbretia 'Lucifer', Gloriosa Daisy. Alternatives: (for spring) Tulip 'Red Emperor', Daffodil 'Primeur'.

echo
the color of one flower

Add interest by repeating colors. Use a

variety of blossom shapes and

sizes, allowing color to provide the unity to

tie it all together. Strive for plants

that bloom at the same time. Plants: *from left:*

Helen's Flower 'Brilliant', Yarrow.

Alternatives: Marigold 'Golden Gem',

Sunflower 'Teddy Bear'.

front -row color

Use tall, somewhat airy plants toward the front of the garden beds and borders. Like a brightly colored veil, this allows visitors to view the rest of the garden through a natural frame of stems and flowers. Plants: *from front:* Maltese Cross, Coreopsis. Alternatives: Bee Balm 'Cambridge Scarlet', Oenothera 'Fireworks'.

The bigger the flower, the more attention it calls to itself. Daylilies, whether in bright bold hues or cooler shades, are always eye-catching. To show them off best, pair them with a smaller flower of a contrasting color. Plants: *from top left:* Daylily, Threadleaf Coreopsis. Alternatives: Lily 'Cancun', False Sunflower.

large flowers offer high impact

experiment

with winning shades of color

Decide on a color combination, then select

other plants with darker or lighter

hues to expand the garden palette. Consider

perennials and shrubs, such as

barberries, for their colorful foliage. Plants:

from left: Shrubby Cinquefoil,

Japanese Barberry. Alternatives:

Chrysanthemum, Heuchera 'Palace Purple'.

increase

the color contrast

The scarlet-tinged leaves of the red-flowered

cockscomb echo its blossoms and

heighten contrast with the yellow marigolds.

Many interesting foliage plants are

now available at local nurseries. Plants: *from*

left: Marigold 'Lemon Drop',

Cockscomb 'Prestige Scarlet'. Alternatives:

Sunflower 'Sunbeam', Giant Wild Parsnip.

opposites attract

Shades of yellow and orange contrast beautifully with hues of purple and blue in this match. As the sun sets and the poppies close up, this combination cools down. Plants: *from top:* California Poppy, Verbena 'Imagination'. Alternatives: Globeflower 'Orange Princess', Sweet Alyssum 'Easter Bonnet'.

soften with pastel hues

For those not accustomed to brash combinations,

pastels produce a gentler look. Even

though the purple here is vivid, the eye is drawn to the

soft peach-colored dahlia first. Plants:

from left: Dahlia 'Betty', Aster 'Purple Dome'. Alternatives:

Dianthus 'Helen', Heliotrope 'Marine'.

eat the
brilliant flowers

Edible flowers, versatile in the kitchen and garden, span the growing season from spring to frost. A delicious pair of favorites blooms together in mild-winter areas in midspring. Plants: *from top:* Calendula, Tulip 'Balalaika'. Alternatives: Marigold 'Tangerine Gem', Nasturtium 'Empress of India'.

Today's coleus are no longer gaudy Victorian plants relegated to the depths of the shade garden. Sophisticated and sun-loving coleus consort well with most garden plants. Plants: *from top:* Coleus 'Wizard Hybrids', Nasturtium 'Alaska Hybrids'. Alternatives: Canna 'Yellow Futurity', Amaranth 'Illumination'.

crazy for coleus

Flamboyant reds and oranges are guaranteed to fuel the flames of any garden. Such "hot" colors provide the illusion of warmth, even in the coolest of climes, and are appreciated early in the season. Plants: *from front:* California Poppy, Red Flax. Alternatives: Black-Eyed Susan Vine, Cardinal Climber.

turn up the heat with fiery colors

foil flowers with foliage

Vibrant red, yellow, and purple blooms benefit from foliage that sets them apart from one another. Without the leaves, this mix would be too riotous for many gardeners. Plants: Coreopsis 'Early Sunrise', Geranium 'Pinto Red', Verbena 'Vervain'. Alternatives: Marsh Marigold, Oriental Poppy, Japanese Iris.

take charge with

chartreuse

This attention-getting greenish yellow says "look at me," radiating light even on sunless days. The bold grass sets off the deep blue campanula flowers, which might otherwise fade into the background. Plants: *from left:* Fairies' Thimble, Hakone Grass. Alternatives: Forget-Me-Not, Yellow Flag Iris.

Though individual penstemon flowers are diminutive, the plants bear so many blossoms that they appear as a solid backdrop of golden yellow. The larger, mauve flowers appear to float atop wiry stems on a sunny sea. Plants: *from left:* Yellow Penstemon, Pincushion Flower. Alternatives: Forsythia, Korean Azalea.

set blossoms adrift

underfoot

Pale yellows and soft shades of violet are

signature colors of the season of

renewal, starting with the very first species

crocus. Electrify the ground level

with a conspiracy of chartreuse and purple

in mid- to late spring. Plants: *from*

top: Cushion Spurge, Woodland Phlox.

Alternatives: Lady's Mantle, Periwinkle.

make joyful color associations

For added dimension, select Japanese iris, whose azure color ranges from palely veined to triumphant blue. As a counterpoint, mix in a few large white and yellow-orange blooms to echo the iris centers. Plants: *from left:* Regal Lily, Japanese Iris, Asiatic Lily. Alternatives: Crocus, Netted Iris, *Tulipa kaufmanniana*.

seek relationships of
tone

Achieve a brilliant effect with the addition

of pastel pink to a sunshine-colored

planting. Pale colors change the perception

of the combination, softening its

dramatic stance. Plants: *from left:* Catmint,

Jupiter's Beard, Yarrow 'Moonshine'.

Alternatives: Balloon Flower, Hollyhock

Mallow, Bloodflower 'Silky Gold'.

savor summer's splendor

Impose the hazy texture of another wonderful veil through which to view a pleasing vignette. Use plants that attract birds and butterflies to delight visitors from midsummer into autumn. Plants: *from left:* Russian Sage, Rudbeckia 'Goldsturm'. Alternatives: Salvia 'Blue Queen', Marigold 'Inca Yellow'.

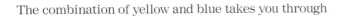

The combination of yellow and blue takes you through

the entire season. Start in spring with this

vivid blue and yellow mix. Keep the marsh marigold from

invading the hyacinth's space. Plants: *from left:*

Marsh Marigold, Grape Hyacinth. Alternatives: Hoop

Petticoat Daffodil, Siberian Squill.

springtime blue and yellow

delicate
flowers with strong color

As dainty and fragile as some blooms may

appear, those with deep, saturated

colors grab and hold attention. Sunny puffs

of yellow against a sky blue

backdrop create a vista evocative of a sunny

afternoon. Plants: *from left:* Siberian

Iris, European Globeflower. Alternatives:

Netted Iris, Danford Iris.

break swaths of color with spikes

Paint with broad sweeps of strong pigment

and punctuate them with a contrasting

color for an exhilarating garden canvas.

Flat lemon yellow yarrow's silvery, fernlike

foliage is spiked with violet-blue

salvia. Plants: *from left:* Yarrow 'Moonshine',

Salvia 'May Night'. Alternatives: Yellow

Cosmos 'Lemon Twist', Cerinthe 'Kiwi Blue'.

vary texture, form, and shape

Along with color, consider texture, form,

and shape. Create an entirely new effect

with the same plants by introducing one

of these elements into the scheme, like

replacing a dominant plant with one that

is light and airy. Plants: *from top:* Yellow

Flag Iris, Catmint. Alternatives: Trout Lily

'Pagoda', Grape Hyacinth 'Blue Spike'.

add a splash of white

Classic design principles suggest incorporating

white or silver to separate blocks

of contrasting colors. A touch of white cools

down vibrant color transitions.

Plants: *from top:* Coreopsis 'Early Sunrise',

Yarrow, Carpathian Harebell

'Blue Clips'. Alternatives: St. John's Wort,

Feverfew, Geranium 'Johnson's Blue'.

interject **cooling** pink

Separating hot orange and blue flowers with soft pink blooms cools down the mix. The pink blossoms dominate the scene as they are larger than the others. Plants: *clockwise from top right:* Milk Vetch, Geum 'Mrs. J. Bradshaw', Siberian Iris. Alternatives: Pink Cardinal Flower, Scarlet Monkey Flower, Bottle Gentian.

pink on the side

The effect is different when the two contrasting flowers are

side by side and you add a muting color

alongside. The light pink daisies lead your eye into the purple

asters. Plants: *from top:* Goldenrod, New

England Aster, Michaelmas Daisy. Alternatives: Scotch

Broom, *Daphne genkwa,* Rhododendron 'PJM'.

try ornamental edibles

The colors and textures of many of the edible greens deserve a front row in the garden. Plant the chard where the early morning or late-afternoon sun shines through the leaves. Plants: *from top:* Kale 'Purple', Kale 'Blond', Chard 'Rhubarb'. Alternatives: Lettuce 'Merlot', Lettuce 'Lollo Bionda', Red Sorrel.

A red and white combination is especially striking in the late afternoon. As the sun slowly sets, the reds begin to glow, while the whites come into their own. For added interest, choose night-fragrant white flowers. Plants: *from top:* Corn Poppy, Flowering Tobacco. Alternatives: Persian Buttercup, Freesia.

focus on red and white

use foliage as a foil

Vibrant colors aren't as stark when set off

by green leaves. Select plants with

green foliage to heighten the complementary

color effects. Plants: *from top:*

Canna 'Ambassador', Abyssinian Gladiolus,

Lily 'Casa Blanca' Alternatives:

Crown Imperial, Summer Snowflake, Tulip

'White Triumphator'.

cultivate the classics

Use pale shades of bold colors, such as chartreuse, in the background to reduce the intensity of other vivid colors in the garden. Plants: *clockwise from top:* Golden Hops, Cranesbill, Creeping Thyme, Lamb's Ears. Alternatives: Golden Oregano, Verbena 'Sissinghurst', Garden Pinks, Snow-in-Summer.

hit the blue notes

A dominant foliage color affects the boldness of a grouping. Cool blues are soothing and provide visual relief. Plants: *clockwise from top:* Butterfly Bush 'Lochinch', Rosemary, Verbena 'Homestead Purple', Cushion Spurge. Alternatives: Chaste Tree, Summer Cypress, Keeled Garlic, Sedum 'Cape Blanco'.

admire strident colors

Yellow and purple combine well, but positioning is important. As an accent to vibrant reds and yellows, purple is on the edge of tastefulness for some. Consider it a color fling before winter. Plants: *from top:* Amaranth 'Joseph's Coat', Violet-Flowered Petunia. Alternatives: Canna 'Tropicanna', Martagon Lily.

Woolly plants are invaluable planting partners for sculptural plants and blossoms. Textural combinations tend to succeed with plants from similar habitats. And the silvery leaves cool down the hot pink flowers. Plants: *from top:* Lamb's Ears, Painted Daisy. Alternatives: Dusty Miller, Cockscomb 'Red Velvet'.

try a textured backdrop

choose plants with similar foliage features

Bold foliage plants, such as coleus, are ideal for repeating colors from one plant to the next. Repeat variegated foliage colors to achieve wild and wonderful combinations. Plants: *from top:* Coleus 'Wizard Mix' (3 plants from seed), Dusty Miller. Alternatives: Hosta 'Paul's Glory', Hosta 'Twilight', Hosta 'Sharmon'.

Silvery leaves are the ideal foil for hot colors as well as pastels. Paired with a single, iridescent color, silver makes it appear even brighter. Planted between two flamboyant colors, silver keeps them from clashing. Plants: *from top:* Ice Plant, Mexican Gem. Alternatives: Painted Daisy, Wormwood.

lower the heat

use pink to brighten dark hues

Some blues and purples are so dark and recessive that they benefit from the contrast provided by a splash of pink. Like gentle strokes from an artist's brush, interweave the plants so their colors play off one another. Plants: from left: Sweet William Catchfly, Larkspur 'Eastern Blues'. Alternatives: Turtlehead, Dayflower.

mass plantings for bold effect

The relative size of plants can enhance or diminish

the effect of a color combination. A mass of

erect flower spikes dominated by taller plants at the back

makes a dramatic statement. Plants: *from top:*

Tree Mallow, Viper's Bugloss. Alternatives: Mallow,

Monkshood 'Bressingham Spire'.

intensify the impact

The intense hues of blue and purple provide an attractive backdrop for hot oranges and rust reds. Complementary colors are only enhanced by proximity to each other—which makes them "pop." Plants: *from front:* Asiatic Lily, Bachelor's Button. Alternatives: Crocosmiflora 'Emily McKenzie', Globe Thistle.

add white to change the scene

Separate the same colors with several white-flowered plants, and the effect is toned down. Plants: *clockwise from top right:* California Poppy, Chamomile, French Lavender, Sweet Alyssum. Alternatives: Exbury Azalea 'Gibralter', Woodland Phlox, Lily-of-the-Valley, *Allium caeruleum.*

frost
the flames

Hot combinations become sweet confections

when given a light coat of pink

frosting. A cool pink makes yellows appear

less brash. Plants: *clockwise from*

top: Painted Daisy, Yellow Corydalis, Maiden

Pinks. Alternatives: Spider Flower

'Pink Queen', Russian Virgin's Bower, Red-

Flowered Creeping Thyme.

take notice with colors in

neon

Electric shades of yellow and magenta make for an eye-popping combination that many would have considered too garish until a few years ago. Don't be afraid to try bold combinations! Anything goes in today's gardens. Plants: *from left:* Kamtschatka Sedum, Freeway Daisy. Alternatives: Lily Leek, Peony 'Kansas'.

The colors are the same here as in the combination above. More leaves show in this grouping, effectively separating the two colors. Plants: *clockwise from top:* Gloriosa Daisy, Threadleaf Coreopsis 'Moonbeam', Petunia 'Purple Wave'. Alternatives: Leopard's Bane, Golden Star, Garland Flower.

temper hot colors with leaves

balance height and color

Be aware of the height of plants when choosing combinations. Notice how this combination is a bit less bold, despite the complementary colors, because the flowers are at different heights. Plants: *from left:* Clustered Bellflower, Maltese Cross. Alternatives: Geranium 'Brookside', Cinquefoil 'Arc-En-Ciel'.

veil with tiny flowers

Consider plants that produce dainty flowers atop wiry

stems that seem to float in a delightful

cloud. Mass plantings make serene veils through which

to view a favorite flower. Plants: *from top:*

Exbury Azalea, Siberian Bugloss. Alternatives: Rose

'Europeana', Garden Forget-Me-Not.

go classic in the springtime

Get a head start in the spring garden with a

timeless combination of blooming

bulbs. Smaller bulbs look lovely when

planted in drifts or masses—

hundreds at a time for best effect. Plants:

from top: Grape Hyacinth, Tulip

'Red Emperor'. Alternatives: Poppy

Anemone (blue and red varieties).

have a late-spring fling

Extend the season and increase the

performance of beds and borders by

interplanting later-blooming plants that

will provide plenty of color as the bulbs'

leaves turn brown and die back naturally.

Plants: *from top:* English Daisy, Garden

Forget-Me-Not. Alternatives: Sweet Pea

'Vibrant Firecrest', Betony 'Superba'.

summer fireworks

Blossoms appear adrift in a foamy sea of

green on plants with airy, fernlike foliage.

Many are generous enough (and sturdy

enough) to allow neighboring plants to

use them for support. Plants: *from left:*

Love-in-a-Mist, Flowering Tobacco 'Nikki

Red'. Alternatives: Pincushion Flower

'Butterfly Blue', Salvia 'Lady in Red'.

produce an optical illusion

Feathery-textured, silvery plants provide the

perfect garden canvas for plantings

of dramatic scarlet flowers. Plants: *clockwise*

from top: Salvia 'Blue Bedder',

Artemisia 'Powis Castle', Cactus Dahlia,

Scarlet Sage 'Flare'. Alternatives:

Morning Glory 'Star of Yelta', Russian Sage,

Lobelia 'Queen Victoria', Pinks 'Brilliancy'.

take it to the color
limit

then vary the placement

Start with red. Then add a pale version—pink.

Go to the dark side with purple (blue

and red make purple). Toss in some yellow for

contrast. The result—a vivid mix

that looks great. Plants: *clockwise from top:*

Calendula, Stock (two colors), Pansy.

Alternatives: Sweet Sultan 'Dairy

Maid', Snapdragon, Godetia 'Amethyst Glow'.

Again the same basic vivid mix of colors

but juxtaposed in a different arrangement.

Plants: *clockwise from top:* Spider Flower

'Pink Queen', Tall Verbena, Canna 'Picasso',

Cockscomb 'Forest Fire Improved'.

Alternatives: Garden Phlox 'Bright

Eyes', Russian Sage 'Filagran', Astilbe

'Red Sentinel', Lily 'Golden Splendor'.

126

FORM FORM FORM FORM FOR

FORM FORM FORM FO

Form encompasses the overall shape of the plant (also known as habit), leaf shape, flower shape, texture, and size. Although, at first glance, the role of form may not be as apparent as color, it plays an equally important role in determining plant combinations. To really see form—without the distraction of color—it would be easier to look at black-and-white photographs, but that's not the reality of gardens. When viewing this section of the book, try to focus on the form of each plant and how it relates to others in the combination. Then look at how color enhances that look. ■ When choosing plants for their form, first decide what the focus will be—the overall plant, the leaves, or the flowers. When considering the entire plant, look at its overall shape and decide whether it is rounded, conical, cylindrical, oval, square, rectangular, or some other general shape. Does it have a strongly vertical growth habit with straight stems, or does it sprawl on the ground? Then address the flowers and/or leaves. Flowers may be single, double, or in a larger group. What looks like a single flower, such as any of the flowering onions, is actually made up of an array of individual florets that forms a large cluster. Plants like delphinium, hollyhock, and foxglove have lots of flowers growing along a single upright stem, while others, like wisteria and Virginia sweetspire, have drooping panicles of blooms. Consider the overall shape and look of the flower or flowering stem—round, star-shaped, spiky, trumpet-shaped, and so on. Visualize the leaf shape—rounded, oval, heart-shaped, swordlike, palmate, or irregular—and the leaf edges—smooth, saw-toothed, spined, or lobed. ■ The final consideration is texture. Like the other components of form, texture can be viewed for the entire plant, or just the leaves or flowers. In terms of the whole plant, the texture is the sum of the leaves, stems, flowers. The texture can vary seasonally, especially for deciduous plants that lose their leaves. From season to season, a different part of the plant is more visible. For instance, a stewartia changes its character in late summer and early fall when the large, white camellialike flowers bloom. Then, after the leaves

SUBTLE FORM

drop, the rugged bark takes center stage. Look at the textural characteristics of each part of the plant. Leaves may be smooth, hairy, glaucous (a fine white, waxy coating that makes them appear blue), rippled, spined, needled, soft, heavily veined, and so on. ■ Noted garden writer Felder Rushing equates choosing plant combinations with making flower arrangements. He suggests that plants fit into one of three overall form categories—rounded, frilly, or spiky. Bearing that in mind, a single-form combination would use all rounded, all frilly, or all spiky plants. A subtle form combination would blend round and frilly, or spiky and frilly together, while the mixture of rounded and spiky would be reserved for bold form combinations. An oversimplification, perhaps, but the theory works. ■ A single-form combination can be very eye-catching, depending on which portion of the form echoes from plant to plant. Use color in different ways to emphasize or minimize the similarities. For example, round flowers of different sizes are more obvious if they're all the same color—if they're both daisylike flowers *and* the same color, then it looks like a mother-daughter duo. The effect of a single-form combination depends on which aspect(s) of form are selected. Flower shape is one of the most obvious combinations, followed by leaf shape. If, for example, leaf texture is the chosen aspect, a casual observer may not recognize that there is a physical characteristic that is common to all of the plants, but will see a grouping that "works." ■ Ornamental grasses have a tremendous range in size, shape, and growing habit—from a gracefully arching, fine-leafed, six-inch-high dwarf blue fescue to a stiffly upright, broad-leafed, eight-foot-tall variegated giant reed. They distinguish themselves when paired with other plants—whether contrasting or complementing them. ■ As you start intermingling plants and paying attention to their form, you'll begin to see them in a brand-new light and appreciate characteristics you never noticed before. Color and form are intertwined—see how different colors reflect the combinations.

BOLD
FORM

Single-form combinations, like single-color combinations, can be exquisitely simple, especially when the flower or plant shape is emulated. Look first to the obvious—such as grouping several daisylike-flowered plants together. Choosing plants with flowers of the same size gives a different effect than planting ones of disparate sizes. Add color to the mix to emphasize or detract from the similarities. ■ Don't overlook texture. A grouping of soft, hairy-leafed plants just makes you want to reach out and stroke the foliage. Such an arrangement is especially appealing to children, while one with spiny plants would be a deterrent to children and pets.

single

FORM FORM FORM FO

tap into green
accents

Don't forget the power of green to punctuate

boldly variegated foliage or masses

of strong color. Try to match the green of

the foliage with the veining or

blossom of neighboring plants. Plants:

from top: Persian Shield,

Plectranthus. Alternatives: Caladium

'Candidum', Elephant's Ear.

Sail across a sea of flower spikes. Mass plantings of spires accentuate their strongly vertical habit. Combine colors for a lush disarray. Plants: *clockwise from top left:* Yellow Foxglove, Siberian Catmint, Salvia 'May Night'. Alternatives: Mealy-Cup Sage 'Catima', Ligularia 'The Rocket', Veronica 'Crater Lake Blue'.

get right to the point

Spiky pointed leaves of varying widths, sizes, and colors make for striking pairings. Select plants whose foliage is interesting for at least three seasons. Plants: *from left:* Long-Leafed Lungwort, Hakone Grass. Alternatives: Narrow-Leaf Hosta, Variegated Velvet Grass.

sprinkle the palette with tiny blooms

Side-by-side plantings of plants with tiny blossoms or leaves create an Impressionistic canvas. Regardless of the palette of colors you choose, the effect will be very airy and delicate. Plants: *from top:* Golden Pearlwort, Kamtschatka Sedum. Alternatives: Irish Moss, Sedum 'Atropurpureum'.

glance at the ground

Before the flowers appear, and after they fade, the leaves of most perennial groundcovers are the stars of the show. Plants with the same leaf shape stand out from one another in bold, contrasting colors. Plants: *from left:* Snow-in-Summer, Golden Oregano. Alternatives: Shortleaf Stonecrop, Yellow Moneywort.

nurture leaves of grass

Grasses, with their similar shapes, cavort well together. Accent different-colored grasses with a dark-leafed plant. Plants: *clockwise from top left:* Penstemon 'Husker's Red', Ribbon Grass, Yellow Meadow Foxtail. Alternatives: New Zealand Flax 'Rubrum', Variegated Bulbous Oat Grass, Leatherleaf Sedge.

use horizontal and vertical leaves

Use cool vertical accents near the front of borders to offset

strident background combinations. The habit

and direction of straight leaves form interesting crisscross

patterns. Plants: *from top:* Tiger Lily, Yellow

Cosmos, Blue Oat Grass. Alternatives: Lily 'Connecticut

King', Bloodflower, Japanese Blood Grass.

keep it light and airy

For a light, airy feel to the garden, commingle plants that have small flowers and aren't very floriferous. Include flowers of different shapes for added interest. Plants: *from top left*: Globe Amaranth 'Strawberry Fields', Mealy-Cup Sage. Alternatives: Yellow Cosmos 'Bright Lights', Salvia 'Strata'.

Ornamental grasses catch the wind, making a distinctive rustling sound. Place them behind plants with light, airy panicles of blossoms that will also sway in the breeze. Plants: *from top*: Porcupine Grass, Astilbe 'Bressingham Beauty'. Alternatives: Feather Reed Grass, Rodgersia 'Rosea'.

catch the breeze

Combine groundcovers with light, airy flowers that don't detract from the leaves. The foliage is the main attraction—it doesn't matter if the flowers bloom at the same time. Plants: *clockwise from top:* Lady's Mantle, Hosta 'Albomarginata', Foamflower. Alternatives: Lily Leek, Italian Arum, Strawberry Geranium.

make a woodland splash

get to the heart
of the matter

Some call it the "banana canna craze"—

using dramatic tropical foliage in

summer gardens. Heart-shaped leaves carry

the theme from the largest to the

smallest leaves. Plants: *from top:* Elephant's

Ear, Caladium, Tuberous Begonia.

Alternatives: Violet-Stem Taro, Hardy

Begonia, Coleus 'Christmas Cheer'.

weave stars and stripes

It's fun to create a visual illusion in the garden. Grow plants with very similar leaves next to one another. When they bloom, it looks like two different flowers are coming from the same plant. Plants: *from top:* Love-Lies-Bleeding, Gloriosa Daisy 'Irish Eyes'. Alternatives: Bloody Cranesbill, Sweet Woodruff.

highlight the heart of the drama

Strongly mottled leaves add vitality to the monochromatic garden or vignette. Select flowers that reflect the shape of the leaves, whether they are standing at attention or in a polite curtsy. Plants: *from top left:* Summer Hyacinth, Calla Lily. Alternatives: Hosta 'Patriot', Variegated Siberian Bugloss.

variations
on a theme

Leaves of the same relative size and shape

tend to commingle well. When they

are related by similar coloration or

variations on a hue, they become a

prize-winning alliance. Plants: *from top left:*

Polka-Dot Plant, Wandering Jew.

Alternatives: Eyelash Begonia, Foamflower.

tempting to touch

The sight of downy leaves triggers an
irresistible urge in plant lovers of all ages
to reach out and touch. Don't be afraid to
touch a tempting leaf or bud, but do so
gently: some plants can't tolerate heavy
stroking. Plants: *from top left:*
Plectranthus, Coleus 'Wizard Velvet'.
Alternatives: Lamb's Ears, Cardoon.

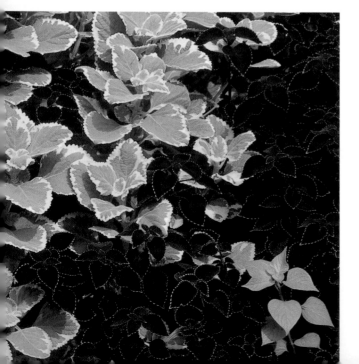

change the color

Use color echoes to mix three plants with similar leaf shapes in the same bed. Consider the triad as two couples who each share a partner—but not the same one. Plants: *from top left:* Variegated Busy-Lizzy, Coleus, Tradescantia 'Purple Heart'. Alternatives: Joseph's Coat, Cuban Oregano, Pennyroyal.

divide
and conquer

Separate look-alike plants, which have

similarly shaped, variegated

leaves, with a distinctly different-looking

plant. Plants: *from top left:*

Variegated Red-Twig Dogwood, Spirea 'Gold

Mound', Hosta 'Albomarginata'.

Alternatives: Cyclamen, Golden Oregano,

Variegated Viola.

encourage curiosity

Succulents and silvery-foliage plants consort well together—both are drought-tolerant and sunloving. When choosing ones with the same form and leaf shape, create interest with plants of contrasting sizes and colors. Plants: *from top left:* Snow-in-Summer, *Echeveria setosa.* Alternatives: Pussytoes, Pork and Beans.

keep it light and airy year-round

Trees and shrubs with airy foliage combine well. Plants:

clockwise from top left: Japanese Maple, Harry

Lauder's Walking Stick, Golden Sawara Cypress, Juniper,

Colorado Blue Spruce. Alternatives: Cut-Leaf

Sumac, Weeping Cherry, Juniper 'Depressa Aurea', Russian

Cypress, Chamaecyparis 'Pembury Blue'.

round out the planting

Achieve harmony in the garden by pairing plants with the same overall form—in this case, round. The effect is heightened when the flower shape echoes that of the entire plant. Plants: *from left:* Perky Sue, Hedgehog Cactus 'Bailey's Lace'. Alternatives: Dahlia 'Slow Fox', Mophead Hydrangea 'Pia'.

Besides repeating color, you can echo any shape found in the garden with an edible plant. Whether spiked, rounded, clustered, or rosette, select only those blossoms that repeat the same shape. Plants: *from top left:* Tulip 'Spring Song', Bok Choy. Alternatives: Nasturtium 'Alaska', Romaine Lettuce 'Olga'.

combine plants tastefully

round
off the edges elegantly

Look at the myriad shapes and forms of

plants and flowers. Suddenly you

discover their similarities and disparities,

revealing the best combinations.

Plants: *from top left:* Zinnia 'Profusion

Cherry', Cabbage 'Tender Sweet'.

Alternatives: Marigold 'Tangerine Gem',

Lettuce 'Great Lakes'.

go for a flat top

Flat-topped flowers provide an air of grace. Think of plants

with distinctive floral elements as dance

partners and pair them with others of a similar habit.

Plants: *from top left:* Shrubby Cinquefoil,

Yarrow 'Paprika'. Alternatives: Lacecap Hydrangea 'Blue

Wave', Variegated St. John's Wort.

tend to the tiny details

Contrast the textured detail of masses or sweeps of petite blossoms with a larger, more conspicuous flower of the same shape. This serves to put each of the partners in perspective. Plants *from top:* Baby's Breath, Yarrow 'Moonshine'. Alternatives: Butterfly Weed 'Hello Yellow', Sweet Autumn Clematis.

For sure-fire success, combine flowers that are similar in form, habit, and color, but are of diverse sizes. When in doubt, use fewer rather than more plants in pairings to maintain a simple association. Plants: *from top:* Gloriosa Daisy, Creeping Zinnia. Alternatives: Sunflower 'Kid Stuff', Zinnia 'Gold Dust Pinwheel'.

mix size and match color

bristling forms

Many flowers change form as they drop

their petals. While in bloom,

petals create their own distinctive form;

afterward the seed heads are the

focal point. Leave some seed heads to attract

birds. Plants: *from top:* Bee Balm

'Raspberry Wine', Globe Thistle.

Alternatives: Lion's Ear, Artichoke.

ring around the rosy
succulents

Many succulents have a beautiful,

symmetrical form—rosettes of

leaves. The overall form may vary somewhat,

but the shared shapes make

successful relationships. Plants: *clockwise*

from top left: Aloe, Delosperma,

Echeveria. Alternatives: Hen-and-Chickens,

Golden Carpet, Cobweb Houseleek.

The textural qualities of two rather disparate-looking plants may be what ties them together well in the garden. Spines, thorns, prickles, and sharp leaves are all strong textural points. They also make effective barriers. Plants: *from top:* Echinopsis, Rockspray Cotoneaster. Alternatives: Cardoon, Wingthorn Rose.

look, but don't touch

Tall spiky flowers can be especially elegant in borders. Arrange several different types of single-stem bloomers according to height for a delightful small-scale tiered effect. Contrasting colors highlight the cascading effect. Plants: *from top:* Mullein, Betony. Alternatives: Foxglove, Jupiter's Beard.

reach for the sky

soften the setting

Plants with soft, hairy leaves just beg to be stroked. The

metamorphosis that plants go through can be

amazing. Once the flowers have faded, some have seedpods

that are like tufts of hair. Plants: *from top left:*

Lamb's Ears, Ceratostigma. Alternatives: Verbascum

'Southern Charm', Russian Virgin's Bower.

find the
central
theme

The similar shapes of flowers and seed

heads make for dynamic partners

in plant marriages. Similar forms and

textures can cause a love to stay,

but contrasting forms and textures carry

the heart away. Plants: *from top:*

Purple Coneflower, Globe Thistle.

Alternatives: Chamomile, Lavender Cotton.

survey the landscape

In a large garden, step back to get a

broad overview of the architecture of the

planting. Suddenly the basic forms and

shapes become readily apparent. Plants,

clockwise from top left: Dietes (out of

bloom), Pride of Madeira, Blue Fescue.

Alternatives: Maiden Grass, Smooth

Hydrangea 'Annabelle', Blue Oat Grass.

get in touch with greens

With the variety in form and color of foliage plants, there's an endless supply of intriguing possibilities for beds and borders. Don't forget to integrate attractive edibles into the overall scheme. Plants: *from left:* Kale 'Redbor', Kale 'Lacinato'. Alternatives: Endive 'Giant Fringed Oyster', Mustard 'Giant Red'.

keep it light and breezy

Loose clusters of nodding flower bells and fine, fernlike foliage create a charming, cottagelike effect. Both leaves and blossoms will sway in the slightest breeze and add another element of interest. Plants: *from top:* Comfrey, Dwarf Lavender Cotton. Alternatives: Virginia Bluebell, French Lavender.

twine flowers and foliage

Noninvasive vines are lovely entwined in shrubs or large perennial plants. When the flower and leaf shapes echo one another, it can be a fun challenge to figure out what goes with what. Plants: *from left:* Clematis 'Nelly Moser', Purple Smokebush. Alternatives: Climbing Fumitory, Dicentra 'Luxuriant'.

prick your interest

Leaves come in all shapes, sizes, colors, and textures. Their edges may be smooth, lobed, serrated, or toothed—some have a surprisingly sharp point. They're beautiful, but keep them away from high-traffic areas. Plants: *from top:* Cardoon, Redleaf Rose. Alternatives: Spiny Bear's Breeches, Chinese Holly.

It's not just the flower or leaf shape that makes a combination work—it's also the plant's overall shape. Plants: *clockwise from top left:* Nasturtium 'Empress of India', Winter Savory, Sweet Alyssum, Marigold 'Lemon Gem'. Alternatives: Miner's Lettuce, Summer Savory, Lemon Thyme, Basil 'Spicy 'Globe'.

round up the herbs

Pair highly textured foliage with highly textured blooms for a

marriage that takes advantage of the overall

form of each plant. Vibrant blossoms contrast well with the

varied leaves of edible greens. Plants: *from left:*

Marigold 'Lemon Gem', Ornamental Kale. Alternatives:

Nasturtium 'Peach Melba', Lettuce 'Red Sails'.

dress it up with frills

sway with ## arching
wands of color

Graceful, arching leaves or stems that reach in every direction are ideal in mixed borders. Combine plants with architectural interest for a special, three-dimensional, soft effect. Plants: *from top:* Rockspray Cotoneaster, Mexican Feather Grass. Alternatives: Japanese Barberry, Leatherleaf Sedge.

Ornamental grasses are among the most fluid of plants. Generally, their leaves aren't stiff, but arch gracefully—in a breeze they look like eddies in a river. Plants: *clockwise from top left:* Pampas Grass 'Sun Stripe', Leatherleaf Sedge. Alternatives: Maiden Grass, Perennial Fountain Grass.

go with the flow

add a feathery touch

Set an informal, romantic mood by pairing
see-through plants with ornamental
grasses. Even as the grasses dry and change
their hues from green to beige, the
overall veil-like effect remains effective.
Plants: *from top left:* Russian Sage,
Mexican Feather Grass. Alternatives: Tall
Verbena, Feather Reed Grass.

One of the easiest ways to come up with a subtle form combination is to start with a single-form combo and put a different spin on it. For example, take the daisylike-flower grouping from single form and substitute a pompom dahlia, football mum, an ornamental kale, or a rose for one of the daisies. Another way to achieve the same effect is to include a plant with round leaves or a spherical habit (no lollipop trees, however). Subtle form combinations are invaluable when creating an entire garden from different combinations. They tie the design together, especially if they draw on characteristics of the single and bold combinations on either side, easing the transition.

subtle

FORM FORM FORM FO

The star-shaped pattern of some flowers, such

as lilies and daylilies, may mimic and harmonize with the

leaf pattern of a nearby plant—a foliage plant

or one that is not in bloom at the same time. Plants:

from top: Lily 'Stargazer', Coleus 'Wizard

Mix'. Alternatives: Lemon Daylily, Ceratostigma.

gaze at the stars

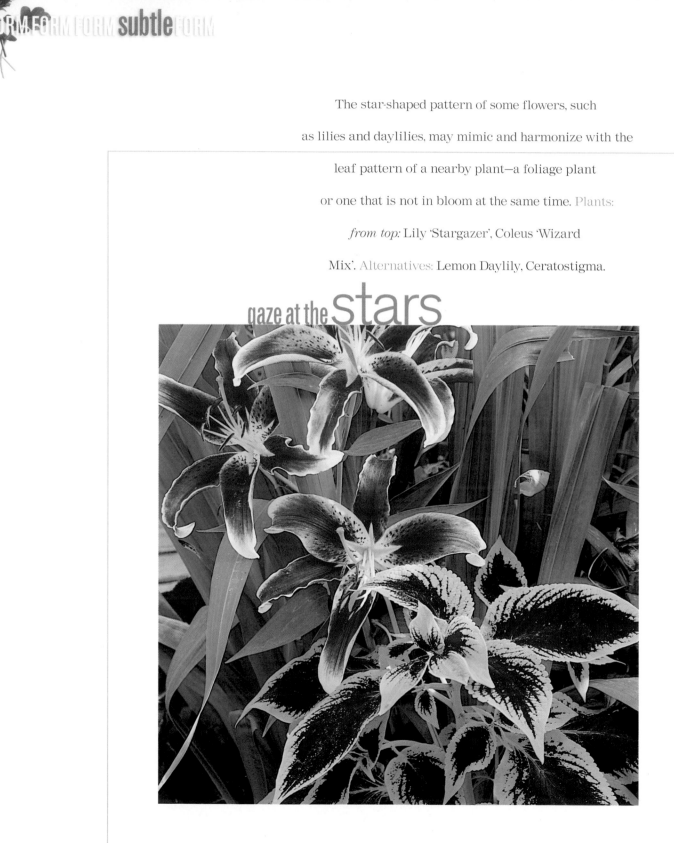

blend in with twining vines

Use vines to blend together similarly shaped leaves of different plants in an artful manner. Plants: *clockwise from top left:* Variegated Japanese Hops, Snow-on-the-Mountain, Coleus 'Wizard Mix'. Alternatives: Variegated Porcelain Berry, Variegated Money Plant, Purple-Leaved Wood Spurge.

plant a living
bouquet

After the kaleidoscope of colors has passed,

remember that form becomes all-

important. Both flower and leaf shapes are

complementary. Plants: *clockwise*

from top left: Spring Starflower, Poppy

Anemone, Jonquil, Tulip.

Alternatives: Sweet Woodruff, Welsh Poppy,

Louisiana Iris, Geum 'Mrs. J. Bradshaw'.

soften the focus with foliage

Bold shapes of color benefit from the inclusion of soft, feathery textures and forms in the foreground. Remember that silvery foliage plants can be used to tone down bright colors. Plants: *from top:* Dame's Rocket, Rabbit Brush. Alternatives: Butterfly Bush 'Royal Red', Wormwood 'Lambrook Silver'.

Blowsy ornamental grasses are another low-key way to tone down strong shapes and colors. For added interest, choose grasses with a variety of different leaf widths and coloration. Plants: *clockwise from top:* Jointed Rush, Douglas Iris, Blue Oat Grass. Alternatives: Dwarf Cattail, Yellow Flag Iris, Variegated Giant Reed.

add grace with grass

weave
a textural
fantasy

Multiple textures can be combined in an

infinite variety of ways to create

easy excitement. Plants: *clockwise from*

top left: Feather Grass,

Russian Sage, Sedum 'Autumn Joy',

Yucca. Alternatives: Pampas

Grass, Mexican Bush Sage, Yarrow

'Paprika', Desert Spoon.

take a good, hard look

When choosing plants at a nursery, put

them on the ground to get a bird's-eye

view of how the shapes mix and match.

Plants: *clockwise from top left:* Hibiscus

'Red Shield', Cigar Flower, Skeleton

Rose Geranium. Alternatives: Castor

Bean 'Scarlet Queen', Honeysuckle 'John

Clayton', Elderberry 'Sutherland Gold'.

launch
a series of shooting stars

Use boldly colored blossoms to attract

attention to the subtleties in

the combinations of the foliage and

flowers. This works equally well at

ground, eye, or tree level. Plants: *from left:*

California Lilac, Cape Weed.

Alternatives: Grape Hyacinth 'Blue

Spike', Leopard's Bane.

admire the fleeting flowers

Enjoy the addition of blooms to the garden, but remember that for many plants, it's the leaf texture and form that dominate most of the year. Plants: *clockwise from top left:* Artemisia 'Powis Castle', Fountain Grass 'Hameln', Silver & Gold. Alternatives: Dusty Miller 'Silver Dust', Pachysandra 'Silver Edge', Northern Sea Oats.

bold backup for airy blooms

The oversize leaves of tender tropical plants are an excellent foil for more delicate blossoms. Choose plants with similarly shaped blooms in disparate sizes. Plants: *from bottom:* Flowering Tobacco 'Lime Green', Gladiola, Canna 'Wyoming'. Alternatives: Beardlip Penstemon, Camas 'Semiplena', Bloodleaf Banana.

set flowers adrift on a silver sea

Choice groundcovers can create an effective canvas against which you can splash larger blooms. Go with flowers that echo the leaf shapes for a sedate look. Plants: *from top left:* Licorice Plant 'Limelight', Verbena 'Homestead Purple'. Alternatives: Dusty Miller 'Cirrus', Heliotrope 'Dwarf Marine'.

roll out the carpet

Allow various groundcovers to battle it out for space in a shady spot. Nestle in a variety of brightly blooming bulbs for varying accents in spring, summer, and fall. Plants: *clockwise from top:* Sweet Woodruff, Lily Leek, Variegated Goutweed. Alternatives: Winter Aconite, Glory-of-the-Snow, Lenten Rose.

provide proper punctuation

Modified star-shaped flowers break up the strong linear

forms that surround them while accentuating

the surrounding radiating lines of foliage and flowers. Plants:

from top: Lavender Cotton, English Lavender,

Daylily 'Perfect Peach Glory'. Alternatives: Sneezewort 'The

Pearl', Salvia 'May Night', Lily 'Dolce Vita'.

command close attention

Diminutive plants can hold their own in the right situation, especially if the larger plant has a light, airy feel to it. The contrast of the colored flowers against the background foliage also draws the eye. Plants: *from top:* Ostrich Fern, Spanish Bluebell. Alternatives: Summer Snowflake, Cinnamon Fern.

Mix, match, and overlap foliage plants with similar shapes and variegation for a lovely textural tapestry. Plants: *from top:* Japanese Painted Fern, Japanese Ginger, Chinese Astilbe 'Pumila', Wild Ginger. Alternatives: Cinnamon Fern, Hosta 'Northern Exposure', Foamflower, Sweet Violet.

produce a mosaic effect

fantasy in the
fronds

Like dainty garden sprites, delicate

blossoms seem to dance among

the lacy fronds of the ferns. At twilight, the

magic happens as the white

flowers flutter gently with the slightest

breeze. Plants: *from left:*

Maidenhair Fern, White Violet. Alternatives:

Royal Fern, Wake Robin.

Curly leaves make a perfect background

for round flowers, as the curled edges echo the flower

shape on a miniature scale. Add a strongly

linear plant for some contrast. Plants: *from top:* Kale

'Winterbor', Leek, Iceland Poppy. Alternatives:

Lettuce 'Green Ice', Garlic, Corn Poppy.

foil flowers with curly leaves

When mixing different leaf shapes—straplike, oval, and scalloped—a gentle segue from one to the other works well. Take into account the role that color plays as well. Plants: *clockwise from top left:* Lily-of-the-Nile (foliage), Lantana, Nasturtium. Alternatives: Spanish Bluebell, Bumald Spirea, Miner's Lettuce.

become an artist in the garden

Take joy in the little and big successes in the garden. Notice how the leaves of one plant echo the flower shape of another. And see how the colors flow smoothly across the garden. Plants: *from left:* Columbine 'McKana Hybrids', Lupine 'Russell Hybrids'. Alternatives: Knap Hill Hybrid Azalea, Merton Foxglove.

celebrate gardening

piece together circles and ovals

Sometimes the best combinations come about by accident. A rejuvenated shrub, pruned back hard in winter, leafs out near ground level the next spring, interacting with other plants. Plants: *from top:* Purple Smokebush, Lungwort. Alternatives: Big Leaf Wintercreeper, Purple-Leaved Wood Spurge.

invite relatives in

One of the easiest ways to come up with a subtle combination is to use two plants that are related in concert with a stranger. Their similarities unify the design. Plants: *from top:* Caladium, Purple Oxalis, Wood Sorrel 'Iron Cross'. Alternatives: Hosta 'Mediovariegata', Wild Columbine, Columbine 'Nora Barlow'.

unveil a silver screen

Tuck lacy foliage plants in among airy flowers of a similar height for a peek-a-boo look in the garden. Plants: *clockwise from left:* Dusty Miller 'Silver Lace', Heliotrope, Blue Salvia, Dusty Miller, 'Silver Dust'. Alternatives: Artemisia 'Powis Castle', Tall Verbena, Monkshood 'Bressingham Spire', Western Mugwort.

move houseplants out into the garden

Many houseplants thrive when planted in the garden for summer. Take cuttings before frost to winter over. Plants: *clockwise from top left:* Variegated Forster's Plectranthus, Variegated Myrtle, Purple Wandering Jew. Alternatives: Ginger Mint, Silver-Edged Lemon Thyme, Sweet Potato Vine 'Blackie'.

let a river run through it

Don't underestimate the unifying effect of a swath of texture or color that runs through and separates clumps of disparate plants. Plants: *clockwise from top left:* Nasturtium 'Alaska Hybrids', Basil 'Red Rubin', Peruvian Daffodil (leaves). Alternatives: Anyu, Purple Perilla, Lily-of-the-Nile (leaves).

take a tropical journey

Bold tropical plants are an ideal—and fast—
way to lend a lush, exotic air to the
home landscape. Dig tender bulbs in fall
before frost, store indoors, then
replant next spring. Plants: *from top:* Coleus
'Beckworth Gem', Golden Calla.
Alternatives: Yellow Archangel 'Herman's
Pride', Jack-in-the-Pulpit.

overlap textures

Allow plants of interest to scramble and intermingle with one another. Pair plants with glossy leaves with matte-finish leaves. If and when the plants flower, it's an added bonus. Plants: *from top:* Variegated Pittosporum, Mediterranean Spurge. Alternatives: Variegated Red-Twig Dogwood, Daphne 'Carol Mackie'.

enjoy the
seasonal success

In spring, as new foliage is emerging, a

perennial combination may have a

totally different look than it does as the

season progresses. Enjoy each

one for its unique qualities. Plants: *from top:*

Spirea 'Gold Flame', Sedum 'Autumn

Joy'. Alternatives: Japanese Photinia,

Hens-and-Chickens 'Sunset'.

echo patterns
and shapes

Look to the vein patterns on leaves to find

inspiration for other plant choices.

Use spiky, bold leaves of a different color to

enhance the subtleties. Plants:

clockwise from top left: Heuchera 'Pewter

Veil', Hakone Grass, Bloody

Cranesbill. Alternatives: Foamflower, Pygmy

Bamboo, Sweet Woodruff.

anchor
feathered finery

Panicles of plumes benefit from the

addition of a saturated

groundcover. Choose a low plant with leaves

that will provide interest

after the long-lasting flowers fade. Plants:

from top: Goatsbeard, *Geranium*

ibericum. Alternatives: Queen-of-the-Prairie,

Lavatera 'Silver Cup'.

add a frosty chill

Fine-toothed fans of "icy" foliage can turn brightly colored, everyday annuals or common perennials into a cool, frosty sensation. Visually, the silver color helps to beat the summer heat. Plants: *from bottom left*: Dusty Miller 'Silver Lace', Heliotrope. Alternatives: White Snakeroot, Wormwood 'Lambrook Silver'.

catch all the
angles

Combine angular plants—those with strong

horizontal or vertical lines. Be sure

that one plant has a lighter visual weight

than the other, or the result may

look like a tic-tac-toe board. Plants: *from left:*

Juniper 'Depressa Aurea', Rose

Campion. Alternatives: False Cypress 'Nana

Aurea', Scotch Thistle.

capture
the seasonal interest

Launch a series of vertical elements to

elevate an ordinary combination

to a more artistic level. Make good use of

the early foliage of summer-

blooming perennials for alliances with

spring bloomers. Plants: *from left:*

Persian Onion, Rudbeckia (foliage).

Alternatives: Chives, Purple Perilla.

paint with tassels of texture

In summer and fall when they send up their flower tassels, ornamental grasses are especially lovely. They add a textural dimension beyond that of the foliage, often softening the allover look. Many will persist through winter. Plants: *from top left:* Purple Fountain Grass, Zinnia. Alternatives: Feathertop, Calendula.

Thick, succulent, colorful, well-leafed stems are still another way to add a vertical element to the garden composition without sacrificing the softness that comes from both the foliage and the flowers. Plants: *from left:* October Daphne, Mazus. Alternatives: Sedum 'Vera Jameson', Golden Oregano.

set off strong stems

plumed foliage
offsets large flower clusters

Gently arching fronds are sure-fire partners

for shrubs with bold clusters of

flowers. The allover shape of the fern leaves

also draws attention to smaller

leaves of the same form. Plants: *from left:*

Azalea, Tassel Fern, Primrose.

Alternatives: Rhododendron 'P.J.M.', Giant

Chain Fern, Celandine Poppy.

Energize large blossoms even further with the inclusion of ornamental grasses. It's great to have movement in the garden. Large flower clusters may be too heavy to catch a breeze, but grasses will. Plants: *from left:* Azalea, Blue Oat Grass. Alternatives: Rose 'Flower Carpet Red', Fountain Grass 'Hameln'.

add motion to the scene

Today's gardeners are getting as bold with their form combinations as they are with color. Tropical plants, which have grown in popularity along with their availability, play a major role in many bold combinations. Their large, almost exaggerated, sizes and shapes (not to mention their colors) are perfect foils for more traditional garden plants. Contrast different textures in the bold realm—from fuzzy leaves to spiny ones, or smooth foliage to heavily veined leaves that appear quilted. The simplest way to make a bold form combination is to set off a round- or oval-leafed plant with one that has spiky foliage, or to contrast a soft form with a hard-edged one.

bold

FORM FORM FORM FO

go for a
tropical look

Use boldly colored, large, open-faced flowers

to infuse the scene with a taste of

the tropics. They contrast well with large,

open spikes of neutral-colored

blooms. Plants: *from top:* Hydrangea

'Tardiva', Hibiscus 'Southern Belle

Hybrids'. Alternatives: Rhubarb 'Valentine',

Clematis 'Ernest Markham'.

find drama in seed heads

Don't be too quick to cut flowers after the blooms have faded. Many have beautiful seed heads that play off other flowers well in the garden. In addition, many seed heads are attractive to birds and butterflies. Plants: *from left:* Montbretia, Russian Globe Thistle. Alternatives: Kaffir Lily, *Allium pulchellum.*

The contrast of tender, exotic, textured leaves against small, brightly colored blooms continues the tropical scene. When the large plants bloom, the effect is enhanced. Plants: *from top*: Lantana 'Miss Huff's Hardy', Naranjilla, Globe Amaranth. Alternatives: Veined Verbena, Datura, Drumstick Allium.

make bigger even better

use high **contrast**
for high style

The large, straplike leaves of some plants

lend a strong sense of geometric

symmetry. Contrast them with a backdrop

of broad, airy blooms for a

very dramatic garden scene. Plants:

from top left: Sedum 'Autumn Joy',

Leek 'Blue Solaise'. Alternatives: Kaffir

Lily, Baby's Breath.

overlay
textures like watercolors

Add variety to the garden by having plants at different levels. A low-growing area gives a different perspective on plants, allowing an overview. Plants: *clockwise from top left:* Hosta, Canadian Hemlock, Strawberry Geranium. Alternatives: Epimedium 'Roseum', Hay-Scented Fern, Sweet Violet.

seek similar growth patterns

Some design concepts are so obvious that they're easily overlooked. Contrast plants with the same growth habit—arching, vertical, or horizontal growing pattern—but with totally different leaf forms, like grasses and ferns. Plants: *from top:* Japanese Painted Fern, Birdfoot Sedge. Alternatives: Japanese Shield Fern, Dwarf Blue Fescue.

Grow two plants with totally disparate shapes and textures together so one appears to come out of the other. Each of their unique characteristics is enhanced more than if they were grown alone as specimen plants. Plants: *from left:* Bamboo, Blue Spruce. Alternatives: Common Horsetail, Japanese Painted Fern.

interject a contrasting form

Show off plants that have a similar leaf patterning but in different proportions. Although the eye is drawn first to the large leaves, it soon notices the more delicate, underlying plant. Plants: *from left:* Variegated Goutweed, Juniper. Alternatives: Variegated Porcelain Berry, Toothed Wood Fern.

magnify the similarities

stand above the crowd

Allow a dainty flowering plant to grow up through a strongly textured foliage plant for a unique illusion. At first glance, it appears to be a single plant, until, upon closer inspection, the color difference is obvious. Plants: *from left:* Lamb's Ears, Geum. Alternatives: Common Sage 'Berggarten', Bonnet Bellflower.

add elusive interest
with allium blossoms

Some members of the onion family have

striking flowers that have an

ephemeral quality. The flower itself may be

fleeting, but its form remains

behind, its color fading through the summer.

Plants: *from top:* Yellow Foxglove,

Star-of-Persia. Alternatives: Delphinium,

Allium 'Globemaster'.

Let the horizontal and vertical lines of plant

stems and leaves distinguish them. Plants: *clockwise from*

bottom left: Lady's Mantle, Foxglove, Hosta

'Frances Williams', Hosta 'Albomarginata'. Alternatives:

Gas Plant, Coralbells 'Mt. St. Helen', Bergenia

'Bressingham Ruby', Variegated Lily-of-the-Valley.

draw divine distinctions

allow border disputes

Let two or three groundcovers or creeping plants duke it out over their territorial borders. The ever-changing boundaries are made all the more fascinating by the size disparity between the plants. Plants: *from top left,* Yellow Moneywort, Golden Pearlwort. Alternatives: Golden Oregano, Irish Moss.

stage an eruption

Plant early bloomers with strong vertical lines and large flowers (in relation to the width of the stems) in a groundcover. They will rise from a sea of low-growing flowers (like a volcano erupting out of the churning ocean). Plants: *from top left:* Daffodil, Wall Rock Cress. Alternatives: Cowslip, Garland Flower.

Plants intermingling with one another give a more carefree look than soldierly rows allow. Like perfect pink bubbles floating on a lacy fabric, small globelike flowers gently meld with ferny, cutleaf-foliage plants. Plants: *from left:* Globe Amaranth, Artemisia 'Powis Castle'. Alternatives: Sea Pink, Dusty Miller.

float flowers in finery

exclaim the virtues of grasses

Allow one of the more diminutive (two feet tall or less)

ornamental grasses to burst out

of a flowering mound. Contrasting colors accentuate the

effusion of the grass. Plants: *from top:*

Hakone Grass, Fairies' Thimble. Alternatives: Variegated

Bulbous Oat Grass, Wishbone Flower.

Light and dark, large and small, simple and intricate, plain and fancy, heart-shaped and filigreed—all these leaf characteristics are best defined in contrast with the others. Plants: *from top:* Japanese Cutleaf Maple, Epimedium. Alternatives: Weeping Serbian Spruce, Caladium 'White Christmas'.

opposites attract

The bold forms of cacti and succulents are unsurpassed by most other plants. Partner ones of contrasting shapes—round or oval with spiky—to make a strong statement in the garden—even with plants of the same color. Plants: *from top left:* Ixote, Indian Fig. Alternatives: Desert Spoon, Dollar Cactus.

contrast strong shapes

Too often vegetables and fruit are relegated to their own neat, rowed dominion. Yet many, especially heirloom varieties, have beautiful texture, form, or color, which should be featured. Plants: *from top left:* Tomato 'Angora', Tricolor Corn, Coleus. Alternatives: Beach Wormwood, Leek, Chameleon Plant.

embrace the chaos

go for the unexpected

Cacti and succulents are traditionally

paired with each other.

Instead, partner one with a delicate annual

or perennial that prefers

the lean, sandy soil in which cacti thrive .

Plants: *from left:* Rock Anise

Hyssop, Cholla. Alternatives: Beardlip

Penstemon, Prickly Pear Cactus.

tout the strong shapes

The new English and French roses, with their classical, full, round flowers, are handsome shrubs that can step out of the traditional rose garden to be paired with lofty perennials. Plants: *from top left:* Delphinium 'Summer Skies', Rose 'Louise Odier'. Alternatives: Breadseed Poppy, Lupine 'Russell Hybrids'.

espouse bold shrubs

Evergreen shrubs are often overlooked in favor of flowers.

Yet they serve the gardener well, with a range

of textures, forms, sizes, and colors that grace the garden

year-round. Plants: *from top left:* Oriental

Arborvitae, Juniper 'Depressa Aurea'. Alternatives: Dwarf

Alberta Spruce, Russian Cypress.

ride the range of shapes

When planning a garden, think like a flower arranger. A combination that includes a rounded, a spiky, and a frilly plant will always look good. Plants: *clockwise from left:* Feather Reed Grass 'Overdam', Heuchera 'Pewter Veil' Bergenia. Alternatives: Variegated Purple Moor Grass, Heucherella, Bok Choy.

reflect
strong
shapes in water

grab everyone's attention

Large, bright bold leaves always command attention. Contrasted with small, delicately filigreed leaves, both are appreciated more for their own unique form, shape, and texture. Plants: *from top left:* Japanese Cutleaf Maple, Hosta 'Frances Williams'. Alternatives: Juniper 'Depressa Aurea', Butterbur.

The reflection of the grounded plants adds another dimension to a water-garden combination. Plants: *clockwise from top left:* Papyrus, Lotus, Jointed Rush, Water Lily 'Charlene Strawn'. Alternatives: Umbrella Palm, Japanese Butterbur, Chinese Water Chestnut, Floating Heart.

know when to

stop

Remember that the young plants that go into the garden now will get bigger. Leave room for their expansion. Plants: *clockwise from top left:* Jupiter's Beard (leaves), Oregano 'Herrenhausen', Silver Sage, Blue Fescue 'Elijah Blue'. Alternatives: Garden Phlox, Sweet Marjoram, Mullein, Birdfoot Sedge.

Set off spherical flowers with a frothy foam of fernlike foliage. Allow contrasting leaves to rise out of the green and show off their unique habit. Contrasting colors add to the beauty of this type of combination. Plants: *from top left:* Fernleaf Tansy, Chives. Alternatives: Rue, Sea Pink.

entice the viewer

combine
evergreens with exotics

Enhance the lush look of broadleaf evergreens

by combining them with large-

leafed plants. Plants: *clockwise from top left:*

Mophead Hydrangea, Rhododendron

(Leaves), Elephant's Ear, Caladium 'June

Bride'. Alternatives: Mountain

Laurel 'Bullseye', Linden Virburnum, Heart-

Leafed Bergenia, Japanese Wild Ginger.

get right to the point

Pairing any of the straight, spiky ornamental grasses makes a strong statement. Add a perennial with bold stems and it's a winner. Plants: *clockwise from top left:* Japanese Blood Grass, Blue Oat Grass, Sedum 'Vera Jameson'. Alternatives: Leatherleaf Sedge, Blue Hair Grass, Mistflower.

surround it with lush foliage

Highlight a vertical element by surrounding it with large-leafed ground-covers. Plants: *clockwise from top left:* Blue Oat Grass, Blue Spruce, New Guinea Impatiens, Bergenia, Hosta 'Gold Standard'. Alternatives: Blue Hair Grass, Chinese Spruce, Rose Periwinkle, Coleus 'Japanese Giant', Caladium.

pour a fountain of grass

A graceful arching form is typical of many of the ornamental grasses. Use them in the garden to emulate water—any type from a waterfall to a fountain, or even a burbling brook. Plants: *from top:* Pampas Grass 'Sunstripe', Gold Juniper, Geranium. Alternatives: Prairie Cord Grass, Moss Rose, Scotch Heather.

make fireworks in the garden

Celebrate the Fourth of July year-round with plants that have strong architectural characteristics resembling a burst of fireworks. Set them off with low-growing, brightly colored, or night-blooming flowers. Plants: *from top:* Sotol, Mexican Evening Primrose. Alternatives: Yucca, Moss Rose.

become an edible artist

Include some of the beautiful edible plants—fruits, vegetables, and edible flowers—in the garden palette. When harvesting, pick only a small portion at a time to extend their time in the garden. Plants: *from bottom left:* Chives, Cabbage 'Sombrero'. Alternatives: Red Clover, Mustard 'Red Giant'.

elevate the senses

For high contrast, choose a strongly vertical plant, such as

many of the ornamental grasses, to set off

plants with flat-topped flowers. Leave the flower heads after

bloom is finished. Plants: *from top:* Feather

Reed Grass 'Stricta', Sedum 'Autumn Joy'. Alternatives:

Japanese Blood Grass, Sneezewort 'The Pearl'.

hang a vertical backdrop

Upright ornamental grasses, in their summer green or autumn beige, shimmer as a backdrop. Plants: *clockwise from top left:* Joe-Pye Weed, Feather Reed Grass, Russian Sage, Rudbeckia 'Goldsturm', Purple Coneflower. Alternatives: Colewort, Zebra Grass, French Lavender, Oxeye Daisy, Painted Daisy.

suspend a SOFT canopy

By contrast, the floppier ornamental

grasses, with their gracefully

arching leaves, add a gentle touch to the

garden. Plants: *clockwise from top:*

Mexican Feather Grass, Zinnia 'Star Orange',

Zinnia 'Star White'. Alternatives:

Maiden Grass, Yellow Cosmos 'Bright

Lights', Yellow Cosmos 'Sunny Red'.

pointed distraction

Large succulents with pointed leaves make a strong architectural statement in the garden. They can also act as a deterrent to pets and children, but may not be safe to have around young, unsupervised children. Plants: *from top:* Muhly Grass, Mescal. Alternatives: Large Blue Fescue, Torch Plant.

try succulence
with spice

Many succulents provide year-round beauty

with leaves—their flowers may

be long-lasting as well. During the growing

season, enhance them with straight-

stemmed perennials with round flowers.

Plants: *from top:* Sedum 'Autumn

Joy', Dianthus 'Red Maiden'. Alternatives:

Pinwheel, Rose Campion.

sprinkle eye candy

The contrast of boldly colored, nearly spherical flowers with ornamental grasses is reminiscent of a handful of jelly beans tossed in the grass of a child's Easter basket. Plants: *from top right:* Perennial Fountain Grass, Zinnia. Alternatives: Meadow Foxtail, Marigold 'Sugar and Spice Mix'.

Use a broad, large shrub or a fast-growing vine as a background plant. Colorful when in bloom, the flowers add form and texture to the mix. Plants: *from top:* Japanese Rose, Blue Fescue, Boxwood 'Kingsville Dwarf'. Alternatives: Lady Banks Rose, Variegated Purple Moor Grass, Japanese Holly 'Convexa'.

frame the perspective

get lost in the haze

Look through the light, airy flowering stems

of many of the smaller

ornamental grasses to see the rest of the

garden. Plants: *clockwise from left:*

Flowering Tobacco, Artemisia 'Powis Castle',

Prairie Dropseed. Alternatives:

Angel's Trumpet, Dusty Miller 'Silver

Lace', Blue Oat Grass.

soften the focus

With their soft plumes of inflorescence,

ornamental grasses in the

front of the garden take away any hard

edges. Plants: *clockwise from top left:*

Miscanthus 'Silver Feather', Flowering

Tobacco, Prairie Dropseed.

Alternatives: Pampas Grass, Butterfly

Weed, Switch Grass.

burst out and **billow** forth

Some plants have an effusive nature. It may be their large,

leaves or their jubilant sprays of airy blooms

that give them an exuberant look. Plants: *clockwise from top*

left: Goatsbeard, Hosta 'Lovepat', Hosta

'Piedmont Gold'. Alternatives: Astilbe 'Snowdrift', Bergenia

'Bressingham Ruby', Siberian Tea.

Enjoy the light that seems to radiate into the rest of the garden from a bold, white-flowered, large-panicled perennial, shrub, or vine early in the season. Plants *from top:* Goatsbeard, Asiatic Lily, Bearded Iris (foliage). Alternatives: Virginia Sweetspire 'Henry's Garnet', Daylily, Blue-Eyed Grass 'Aunt May'.

backlight the scene

find the odd couple

Instead of creating pairings by growing

plants side by side in the garden,

interplant them so they interact more with

each other. The results are often

surprisingly handsome mixes. Plants: *from*

top left: Miniature Fan Palm,

Beefsteak Plant. Alternatives: Umbrella

Plant, Joseph's Coat 'Versicolor'.

explore new worlds

Get more of a sense of depth from statuesque plants with spherical flowers by planting them in front of a small-leafed shrub or tree with a deeper hue. Plants: *from top:* Purpleleaf Sand Cherry, Giant Allium, Lamb's Ears. Alternatives: Burning Bush, Chrysanthemum 'Yellow John Hughes', Toad Lily.

Consider aromatic culinary herbs, whose scents are released by brushing the leaves in passing, for the front of the garden. Plants: *from top:* Basil 'Purple Ruffles', Marigold 'Little Hero Yellow', Basil 'Finissimo Verde a Palla'. Alternatives: Purple Perilla, Calendula 'ButterCreams Mix', Lemon Thyme.

paint an aromatic picture

Within this section is a thumbnail sketch of each of the plants shown in the preceding six chapters. All of the alternative plants given for each combination are also included here. Just look up any of the plants by its common name. The botanical name is given, so that you can readily identify the plant in mail-order catalogs or nurseries—common names can vary around the country. The type of plant (annual, perennial, bulb, tree, shrub, etc.), height, time of bloom, color of flower, hardiness zones, and sun or shade requirements round out the basics for each plant. This is all the information you'll need to decide whether or not a plant is suitable for *your* garden.

index

SCRIPTION DESCRIPT

A

Abyssian Gladiolus (Acidanthera)
Gladiolus callianthus
Bulb; 3'; summer toautumn; white with mahogany throat; fragrant; sun; zones 7–10; *p. 111*

Acacia 'Prostrata'
Acacia redolens 'Prostrata'
Evergreen shrub; 1–2'; spring; yellow; sun; zones 9–10; *p. 76*

Ageratum (Flossflower)
Ageratum houstonianum
Annual; 6–8"; summer tofrost; blue, lavender; sun to part shade; *p. 75*

Allium caeruleum
Bulb; 12–24"; late spring; blue; sun to part shade; zones 2–7; *p. 119*

Allium 'Globemaster'
Bulb; 32"; summer; deep violet; sun; zones 5–9; *p. 207*

Allium karataviense
Bulb; 6–12"; late spring; silvery lilac; mottled gray green leaves; sun to part shade; zones 4–8; *pp. 46, 72*

Allium pulchellum
Allium carinatum subsp. *pulchellum*
Bulb; 12–18"; midsummer; rich purple; sun; zones 6–9; *p. 202*

Aloe
Perennial succulent; 2–7'; winter, spring; white, yellow, orange, red; sun; zones 9–10; *pp. 26, 156*

Amaranth (Summer Poinsettia)
Amaranthus tricolor
Annual; 2–5'; brilliaintly multicolored leaves; sun.
• 'Illumination': 4–5'; crimson and gold leaves; *pp. 24, 96*
• 'Joseph's Coat': 2–3'; gold and crimson upper leaves, brown lower leaves; *pp. 24, 114*

Anemone Clematis
Clematis montana
Deciduous woody vine; 6–10'; late spring through early summer; white; sun to light shade; zones 5–8; *p. 63*

Angel's Trumpet
Datura innoxia (*D. meteloides*)
Annual; to 3'; summer to frost; white to pinkish lavender, single or double; sun to part shade; *p. 231*

Anyu
Tropaeolum tuberosum
Perennial vine; 6–12'; midsummer to fall; scarlet and yellow; sun to part shade; zones 8–10; *p. 188*

Artemisia 'Powis Castle'
Artemisia arborescens 'Powis Castle'
Perennial; 2–3'; lacy, silver leaves; full sun; zones 6–8; *pp. 49, 125, 176, 186, 210, 231*

Artemisia 'Silver King'
Artemisia ludoviciana 'Silver King'
Perennial; 2–3'; silvery gray leaves; sun; zones 3–9; *p. 73*

Artichoke
Cynara scolymus
Perennial vegetable; to 6'; early fall; purple; summer harvest of flower buds; sun; zones 8–9; *p. 156*

Asiatic Lily
Lilium spp. and cvs.
Bulb; perennial; summer to early fall; various colors; sun to part shade; zones 3–10; *pp. 102, 119, 233*
• 'Connecticut King': 3'; yellow; *p. 35*
• 'Enchantment': 2–3'; orange with black spots; *p. 31*

Aster × frikartii
Perennial; 2–3'; summer; lavender blue; sun; zones 5–8; *p. 57*

Aster 'Purple Dome'
Perennial; 18–30"; summer to fall; purple; sun; *p. 95*

Astilbe
Perennial; 1–4'; spring to summer; various colors; part shade to sun; zones 4–8; *p. 67*
• 'Bressingham Beauty' (*A. × arendsii* 'Bressingham Beauty') : 36"; bright pink; midsummer; *p. 141*
• 'Peach Blossom' (*A. japonica* 'Peach Blossom'): 2–3'; salmon pink; *p. 86*
• 'Red Sentinel' (*A. j.* 'Red Sentinel'): 3'; deep red; *pp. 27, 126*
• 'Snowdrift' (*A. simplicifolia* 'Snowdrift'): 2'; bright white; *p. 232*
• 'White Gloria' (*A. × arendsii* 'Weisse Gloria'): 2'; white; *p. 40*

Aurinia corymbosum
Perennial; 12–18"; late spring to midsummer; bright yellow; sun; zones 7–9; *p. 33*

Azalea
Rhododendron spp.
Deciduous or evergreen shrub; 5–7'; late spring; white, pink to scarlet; full to part shade; zones 5–8; *pp. 196, 197*

B

Baby's Breath
Gypsophila paniculata
Perennial; 2–4'; summer; white; sun; zones 3–7; *pp. 75, 153, 203*
• 'Gypsy': annual; 10"; pink; *p. 36*

Bachelor's Button
Centaurea cyanus
Annual; 10–30"; summer; blue, white, pink, purple, red; sun to part shade; *p. 119*

Balloon Flower
Platycodon grandiflorus
Perennial; 18–30"; summer; blue, white, pink; sun to part shade; zones 3–10; *p. 103*
• 'Komachi': 1–2'; clear blue; *p. 85*

Bamboo
Bambusa spp.
Evergreen, clump-forming; 10–50'; green, lance-shaped leaves; sun or part shade; zones 8–10; *p. 205*

Basil
Ocimum basilicum
Annual herb; 12–24"; summer; white or pink; edible flowers; aromatic green leaves; sun.
• 'Finissimo Verde a Palla': 10" globe form; tiny scented leaves; *p. 235*
• 'Purple Ruffles': 24"; purple leaves with ruffled edges; *pp. 67, 235*
• 'Red Rubin': 18"; deep purple leaves; *p. 188*
• 'Spicy Globe': 6"; tiny leaves, rounded growth habit; *p. 164*

Basket-of-Gold
Aurinia saxatilis
Perennial; 12"; spring; vivid yellow; sun; zones 3–7; *p. 33*

Beach Wormwood
Artemisia stellariana
Perennial; 15–24"; summer; yellow; silver leaves; sun; zones 4–8; *pp. 49, 213*

Bearded Iris
Iris hybrids
Perennial; 8–36"; early summer; various colors; sun to part shade; zones 3–10; *pp. 51, 233*

Beardlip Penstemon
Penstemon barbatus
Perennial; 18–36"; late spring to fall; pink to carmine red; sun to part shade; zones 3–9; *pp. 177, 213*

Bear's Breeches
Acanthus mollis
Perennial; 30–48"; late spring; purple; sun to part shade; zones 7–9; *p. 45*

Bee Balm
Monarda didyma
Perennial; 30–36"; summer; red; edible flowers; sun to part shade;

zones 4–10.
- 'Aquarius': 2–3'; light pink; *p. 73*
- 'Cambridge Scarlet': 3'; red; *p. 92*
- 'Gardenview Scarlet': 30–42'; large deep red; *p. 27*
- 'Raspberry Wine': 30–42'; wine red; mildew-resistant; *p. 156*

Beefsteak Plant
Iresine herbstii 'Brilliantissima'
Annual; to 5'; rich crimson leaves with purplish markings; sun to part shade; *p. 234*

Bergamot
Monarda fistulosa
Perennial; 2–5'; late summer; lilac; sun to part shade; zones 3–7; *p. 83*

Bergenia
Evergreen perennial; 12–18"; early spring; white, pink, red; part shade or sun; zones 3–8; *pp. 217, 223*
- 'Bressingham Ruby': 14"; red flowers, new leaves; *pp. 208, 232*

Betony
Stachys macrantha
Perennial; 1–2'; late spring; violet; sun to part shade; zones 2–8; *p. 158*
- 'Superba': 2'; rosy pink; *p. 125*

Big Leaf Wintercreeper
Euonymus fortunei 'Vegetus'
Evergreen shrub; 4–5'; can grow as a climber to 15'; dark green, glossy leaves; pink to red fruits; sun or part shade; zones 4–8; *p. 186*

Birdfoot Sedge
Carex conica 'Variegata'
Evergreen perennial; 6–15"; green and white grassy leaves; sun or part shade; zones 5–9; *pp. 204, 220*

Black-Eyed Susan Vine
Thunbergia alata
Annual vine; 6'; summer through fall; gold, yellow, or white, with dark throat; sun to part shade; *p. 97*

Black Mondo Grass
Ophiopogon planiscapus 'Arabicus'
Evergreen perennial; 6"; summer; lilac to pink; leaves nearly black; sun to part shade; zones 6–10; *p. 55*

Blanket Flower 'Dazzler'
Gaillardia grandiflora 'Dazzler'
Perennial; 2–3'; summer; orange red centers and petals, with yellow tips; sun; zones 2–9; *p. 33*

Bloodflower
Asclepias curassavica
Subshrub grown as an annual; 3'; summer to fall; red, orange, yellow; full sun; zones 9–10; *p. 140*
- 'Silky Gold': golden yellow; *p. 103*

Bloodleaf Banana
Musa acuminata 'Sumatrana'
Perennial; 6–8'; leaves splashed and streaked with wine red; sun to part shade; Zone 10; *p. 177*

Bloody Cranesbill
Geranium sanguineum
Perennial; 9–12"; spring to summer; magenta pink; sun to part shade; zones 3–8; *pp. 145, 191*
- 'Album': 10–18"; white; *p. 61*

Bluebeard
Caryopteris × *clandonensis*
Deciduous shrub; 3'; summer to fall; blue; full sun to part shade; zones 5–8; *p. 65*

Blue-Eyed Grass 'Aunt May'
Sisyrinchium striatum 'Aunt May'
Perennial; to 20"; early to midsummer; pale yellow; irislike leaves striped creamy yellow; sun; zones 7–8; *p. 233*

Blue-Eyed Mary
Omphalodes verna
Semievergreen perennial; 8"; spring to early summer; dark blue with white eye; shade; zones 6–9; *p. 60*

Blue False Indigo
Baptisia australis
Perennial; 3–4'; early summer; blue; sun to part shade; zones 3–10; *p. 65*

Blue Fescue
Festuca glauca
Perennial; 6–10"; summer; blue green with violet flush; silvery blue leaves; sun to light shade; zones 4–8; *pp. 73, 160, 231*
- 'Elijah's Blue': 12"; soft blue leaves; *p. 220*

Blue Hair Grass
Koeleria glauca
Perennial; 16"; summer; silver green, aging to buff; glaucous gray green leaves; sun to part shade; zones 6–9; *p. 223*

Blue Lyme Grass
Leymus arenarius (*Elymus glaucus*)
Perennial; 2–3'; silver blue leaves; sun; zones 5–9; *p. 79*

Blue Oat Grass
Helictotrichon sempervirens
Perennial; 24–30"; summer to fall; tan flowers, blue gray leaves; sun; zones 4–9; *pp. 140, 160, 173, 197, 223, 231*

Blue Salvia
Salvia farinacea
Perennial, usually grown as an annual; 14–30"; summer through fall; blue; sun to part shade; zones 8–10; *p. 186*
- 'Victoria': 18"; deep blue; *p. 74*

Blue Spruce
Picea pungens glauca
Evergreen tree; 12–60'; bluish silver leaves; sun; zones 2–7; *pp. 205, 223*

Bok Choy
Brassica rapa, Chinensis group
Annual vegetable; 8–20"; spring and fall; white stalks, dark green leaves; sun to part shade; *pp. 78, 150, 217*

Boltonia
Boltonia asteroides
Perennial; 3–6'; late summer to fall;

white; sun to part shade; zones 4–8; *p. 68*

Bonnet Bellflower
Codonopsis convolvulacea
Perennial vine; to 6'; summer; violet blue to white; sun to part shade; zones 5–9; *p. 206*

Bottle Gentian
Gentiana andrewsii

Perennial; 16–30"; fall; deep blue; sun; zones 3–7; *p. 108*

Bowles Golden Grass
Carex elata 'Bowles Golden'
Perennial sedge; 2–3'; leaves golden yellow with green margins; part shade or sun; zones 5–9; *p. 38*

Boxwood 'Kingsville Dwarf'
Buxus microphylla var. *japonica*

'Kingsville Dwarf'
Evergreen shrub; 24"; dark green leaves turns bronze over winter; compact and slow-growing; part shade or sun; zones 6–9; *p. 230*

Breadseed Poppy
Papaver somniferum
Annual; 3–4'; early summer; pink, white, mauve, red to almost black; sun or light shade; *pp. 72, 215*

Broadleafed Penstemon
Penstemon ovatus
Perennial; 2–4'; summer; purple blue, indigo; sun; zones 3–9; *p. 80*

Brown-Eyed Susan
Rudbeckia triloba
Perennial; 2–3'; summer to fall; yellow with purplish black centers; sun; zone 3–10; *p. 34*

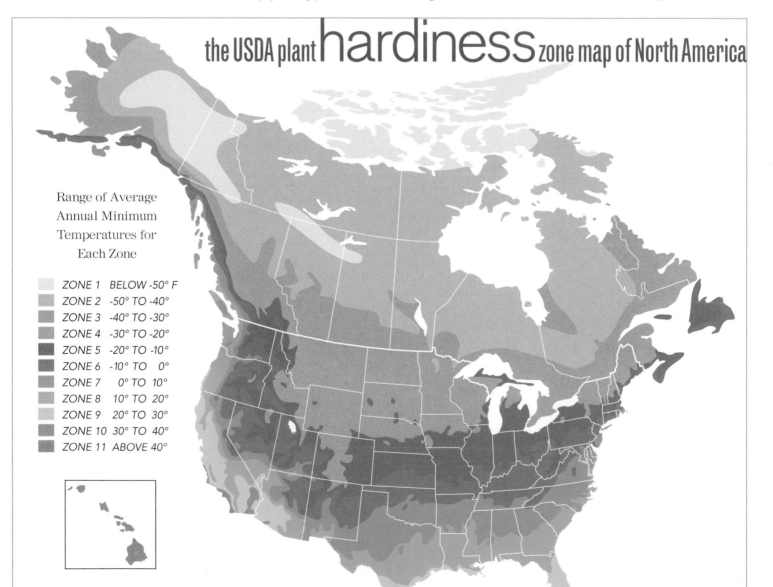

the USDA plant **hardiness** zone map of North America

Range of Average Annual Minimum Temperatures for Each Zone

	ZONE 1	BELOW -50° F
	ZONE 2	-50° TO -40°
	ZONE 3	-40° TO -30°
	ZONE 4	-30° TO -20°
	ZONE 5	-20° TO -10°
	ZONE 6	-10° TO 0°
	ZONE 7	0° TO 10°
	ZONE 8	10° TO 20°
	ZONE 9	20° TO 30°
	ZONE 10	30° TO 40°
	ZONE 11	ABOVE 40°

Bugleweed
Ajuga reptans
Perennial; 4–12"; late spring; blue; sun or shade; zones 3–9; *p. 71*

Bumald Spirea
Spiraea japonica 'Bumaldi'
Deciduous shrub; 3'; summer; deep pink flowers; new leaves bronze, turning green; sun or part shade; zones 4–8; *p. 183*

Burkwood Viburnum
Viburnum burkwoodii
Deciduous shrub; 8'; spring; white, fragrant; sun or part shade; zones 4–8; *p. 43*

Burning Bush
Euonymus alatus
Deciduous shrub; 15–20'; dark green leaves turn brilliant reddish pink in fall; sun; zones 4–9; *p. 235*

Butterbur
Petasites hybridus
Perennial; 1–2'; late winter to early spring; purple; sun to part shade; zones 4–8; *p. 219*

Butterfly Bush
Buddleia davidii and cvs.
Deciduous shrub; 10–15'; summer to frost; lilac to purple; fragrant; sun to part shade; zones 6–9.
• 'Lochinch': 8'; lavender blue with orange eyes; *p. 113*
• 'Royal Red': dark red-violet; *p. 173*

Butterfly Weed
Asclepias tuberosa
Perennial; 24–30"; midsummer to fall; orange; sun to part shade; zones 4–9; *p. 231*
• 'Hello Yellow': yellow; *p. 153*

C

Cabbage
Brassica oleracea, Capitata group
Vegetable; 70–90 days; spring, fall harvest; green, red purple; sun
• 'Early Jersey Wakefield': 65 days; small, pointed heads; heirloom variety; *p. 78*
• 'Sombrero': 67 days; red cabbage with compact heads; *p. 224*
• 'Tender Sweet': 71 days; flat, green heads; remain tender, without splitting, 5–7 weeks; *p. 151*

Cactus Dahlia
Dahlia hybrids
Bulb; 1–7'; summer to fall; large sunburst shaped flowers with pointed tips; various colors and bicolors; sun; zones 8–11; *pp. 28, 31, 125*

Caladium
Caladium bicolor
Bulb; 1–3'; summer to fall; beautiful colored leaves; part to full shade; zones 10–11; *pp. 143, 186, 223*
• 'Candidum': silvery white leaves with green variegation; *p. 136*
• 'Cardinal': 18"; rich crimson leaves edged with green; *p. 25*
• 'June Bride': silvery white, green veined and edged leaves; *p. 221*
• 'Little Miss Muffet': 8–12"; lime green leaves with burgundy speckles and veins; *p. 50*
• 'Sweetheart': 15"; white leaves with pink flushing and veins, green edges; *p. 55*
• 'White Christmas': 21"; silvery leaves with green veins; *p. 213*

Calamondin Tree
Citrofortunella microcarpa
Evergreen shrub; 10–20'; spring to summer; white, fragrant; orange fruit; sun; zones 10–11; *p. 33*

Calendula (Pot Marigold)
Calendula officinalis
Annual; 12–30"; summer to fall; yellow to orange; edible flowers; sun; *pp. 96, 126, 195*
• 'ButterCreams Mix': large, prominent centers; shades of cream, yellow, gold, apricot, orange; *p. 235*

California Lilac
Ceanothus spp.
Shrub; 2–10'; spring; blue, purple; sun; zones 8–10; *p. 176*

California Poppy
Eschscholzia californica
Annual; 8–12"; summer to frost; orange; sun; *pp. 69, 94, 97, 119*

Calla Lily
Zantedeschia albomaculata.
Bulb; 1–4'; summer to fall; white to cream; arrow-shaped leaves with white spots; sun or part shade; zones 8–11; *p. 145*

Camas
Camassia leichtlinii
Bulb; 3–4'; early summer; white, blue, purple; sun to part shade; zones 5–9; *p. 65*
• 'Semiplena': semidouble, creamy white; *p. 177*

Campanula garganica
Perennial; 5–6"; spring; blue; sun to part shade; zones 5–7; *p. 55*

Canadian Hemlock
Tsuga canadensis
Evergreen tree; to 90'; fine, dark green needles; sun or part shade; zones 3–7; *p. 204*

Canary Creeper
Tropaeolum peregrinum
Annual vine; 8–12'; summer to fall; yellow; sun to part shade; *p. 33*

Candytuft
Iberis sempervirens
Evergreen perennial; 9–12"; spring; white; sun; zones 3–8; *p. 60*

Canna
Canna × generalis
Bulb; 2–6'; summer to frost; various colors of flowers and leaves; sun; zones 7–10.
• 'Ambassador' ('Black Knight'):

cacti and succulents for dry climates

Aloe
Cholla
Cleistocactus
Cobweb Houseleek
Delosperma
Desert Spoon
Dollar Cactus
Echeveria
Echinopsis
Golden Carpet
Hedgehog Cactus
Hens-and-Chickens
Ice Plant
Indian Fig
Kamtschatka Sedum
Mescal
Mexican Gem
October Daphne
Pinwheel
Pork and Beans
Prickly Pear Cactus
Sedum 'Atropurpureum'
Sedum 'Autumn Joy'
Sedum 'Cape Blanco'
Sedum 'Honey Song'
Sedum 'Moonglow'
Sedum 'Rosy Glow'
Sedum 'Vera Jameson'
Shortleaf Stonecrop
Torch Plant

add a tree for shade

Blue Spruce
Canadian Hemlock
Chamaecyparis 'Pembury Blue'
Chaste Tree
Chinese Holly
Chinese Spruce
Colorado Blue Spruce
Desert Spoon
Japanese Cutleaf Maple
Japanese Maple
Meyer Lemon
Miniature Fan Palm
Weeping Cherry
Weeping Serbian Spruce

Cleistocactus
Cactus; 3–5'; spring to summer; yellow, red, orange; sun; zones 9–10; *p. 26*

Clematis
Woody vine; 6–10'; late spring to midsummer; white, pink, red, or purple; sun; zones 5–9.
• 'Ernest Markham': red violet with velvety sheen; *p. 200*
• 'Nelly Moser': mauve pink with darker bands; *p. 163*

Cliff-Green
Paxistima canbyi
Evergreen shrub; 16", spreading; leaves glossy dark green; sun to part shade; zones 3–7; *p. 44*

Climbing Fumitory
Adlumia fungosa
Biennial vine; 10–15'; summer to fall; pale pink, white; sun or part shade; zones 6–9; *p. 163*

Clustered Bellflower
Campanula glomerata
Perennial; 1–3'; early to midsummer; blue, purple; sun to part shade; zones 3–8; *p. 122*

Cobweb Houseleek
Sempervivum arachnoideum
Succulent perennial; 3", spreading; summer; reddish pink; leaf rosettes cobwebbed with white hairs; sun; zones 5–8; *p. 156*

Cockscomb
Celosia argentea
Annual; summer to frost; yellow, orange, red, pink; full sun
• 'Forest Fire Improved' (*C. a.* var. *plumosa* 'Forest Fire Improved'): 24"; orange scarlet, plumed; bronze leaves; *p. 126*
• 'Prestige Scarlet' (*C. a.* var. *cristata* 'Prestige Scarlet'): 18"; red, crested; *p. 93*
• 'Red Velvet' (*C. a.* var. *cristata* 'Red Velvet'): 24–30"; crimson, crested; *p. 114*

Coleus
Solenostemon scutellariodes
Perennial, usually grown as an annual; 2–3'; colorful leaves; sun to part shade; zone 10; *pp. 147, 213*
• 'Alabama Sunset': 36"; deep pink with yellow flushing; *p. 70*
• 'Antique': coppery green leaves with brick rose speckling; *p. 27*
• 'Beckworth Gem': to 28"; burgundy with purple center, gold margins; *p. 189*
• 'Christmas Cheer': to 18"; splashes of red, cream, and yellow; *p. 143*
• 'Eclipse': to 24"; brilliant violet leaves blushed pinkish rose; *p. 27*
• 'Flair': 24"; deep red with green edging; *p. 27*
• 'Gay's Delight': 30"; chartreuse leaves with purple veining; sun-loving; *p. 24*
• 'Japanese Giant': to 42"; large burgundy leaves with scalloped light green edges; *p. 223*
• 'Limeline': 24–30"; chartreuse leaves with burgundy vein; *p. 38*
• 'Mardi Gras': to 24"; compact; gold green leaves splashed carmine, pink, and pastel brown; *p. 27*
• 'Pineapple Queen': 24"; chartreuse with dark purple veins; *p. 39*
• 'Rob Roy': 15–30"; pink and purple leaves with green edges; *p. 55*
• 'Wine and Lime': 36"; chartreuse leaves with large burgundy markings; sun-loving; *p. 24*
• 'Wizard Hybrids': 10–12"; various colors and blends; *pp. 27, 96, 115, 170, 171*
• 'Wizard Velvet': 10–12"; dark velvety red with thin gold serrated edge; *p. 146*

Colewort
Crambe cordifolia
Perennial; 4–7' tall, 5' wide; summer; clouds of white flowers; sun; zones 5–8; *p. 226*

Colorado Blue Spruce
Picea pungens glauca
Evergreen tree; 12–60'; silvery blue needles; sun;

zones 2–7; *pp. 149, 205*

Columbine
Aquilegia spp.
Perennial; 8–24"; spring to early summer; various; part shade to sun; zones 3–9.
• 'McKana Hybrids': 18–24"; various colors, long-spurred; *p. 185*
• 'Nora Barlow'(*A. vulgaris* 'Nora Barlow'): 24–30"; pink with white, fully double; *p. 186*

Comfrey
Symphytum officinale
Perennial herb; 3–4'; white, pink, lavender; sun to part shade; zones 4–7; *p. 163*

Common Fleabane
Erigeron philadelphicus
Perennial; 18–30"; early summer; whitish pink; sun to part shade; zones 3–8; *p. 75*

Common Horsetail
Equisetum hyemale
Aquatic perennial; to 4', spreading; green jointed stems with black bands; sun; zones 3–11; *p. 205*

Common Sage
Salvia officinalis
Perennial herb; 12–24"; summer; purple; edible flowers; silver aromatic leaves; sun, light shade; zones 4–9; *p. 60*
• 'Berggarten': deep blue flowers; gray green leaves; *p. 206*
• 'Icterina': non-flowering; variegated yellow and green leaves; zones 7–8; *p. 38*

Coneflower 'Herbstonne'
Rudbeckia nitida 'Herbstonne'
Perennial; 5–7'; late summer to fall; yellow; sun; zones 3–9; *p. 85*

Copperleaf
Acalypha wilkesiana 'Marginata'
Tender shrub; 3–6'; multicolored leaves, with crimson to white edges; sun to part shade; zone 10; *p. 29*

Succulent perennial; 2–5"; summer; orange, red, purple; sun; zones 9–10; *p. 156*

Delphinium
Delphinium elatum
Perennial; 3–8', spring to summer; blue to white; sun or light shade; zones 3–10; *p. 207*
• 'Blue Springs': 3–5'; deep blue with dark eyes; *pp. 73, 79*
• 'Connecticut Yankee': 3–4'; single white, blue, mauve; *pp. 48, 140*
• 'Pacific Giant Hybrids': 3–6'; various colors; double flowers; *p. 86*
• 'Summer Skies': double blue with white center; *p. 215*

Desert Spoon
Dasylirion wheeleri
Evergreen tree; 11–20'; summer; 5' spikes of white flowers; sun; zones 9–10; *pp. 174, 213*

Dianthus
Perennial; 8–24"; spring to early summer; pink, white, red; edible flowers; sun; zones 3–8; *p. 57*
• 'Helen': 10–18"; summer; deep pink; fragrant; evergreen, blue green leaves; zones 4–8; *p. 95*
• 'Ipswich Pinks': 9"; white, red, pink; fragrant; blue green leaves; *p. 87*
• 'Red Maiden' (*D. deltoides* 'Red Maiden'): 6"; reddish purple; good heat tolerance; zones 3–8 *p. 229*

Dicentra 'Luxuriant'
Perennial; 12–15"; spring to summer; cherry red; ferny leaves; part shade, sun; zones 4–8; *p. 163*

Dietes
Perennial; 3–4'; spring to summer; white with brown markings; sun to part shade; zones 9–11; *p. 160*

Dollar Cactus (Purple Prickly Pear)
Opuntia violacea 'Santa Rita'
Cactus; 6'; spring to summer; yellow; leaves are purple flushed with

maroon edges; sun; zones 9–11; *pp. 76, 213*

Douglas Iris
Iris douglasiana
Evergreen perennial; 6–28"; late spring to early summer; various colors; sun or part shade; zones 7–9; *p. 173*

Dracaena 'Tricolor'
Dracaena cincta 'Tricolor'
Evergreen shrub; 6–15'; dark green leaves edged cream and red; *p. 29*

Drumstick Allium
Allium sphaerocephalum
Bulb; 18–36"; late spring; purple; sun; zones 4–8; *p. 202*

Dusty-Miller
Centaurea cineraria
Evergreen subshrub grown as an annual; 8–24"; finely cut, silvery, felted leaves; sun; zones 7–9; *p. 210*

Dusty Miller
Senecio cineraria
Perennial grown as an annual; 18–30"; silvery gray leaves; sun; zones 4–10; *pp. 114, 115*
• 'Cirrus': 6–8"; rounded silver leaves; *p. 177*
• 'Silver Dust': 8"; finely cut silver leaves; *pp. 67, 176, 186*
• 'Silver Lace': 10"; lacy, silver leaves; *pp. 186, 193, 231*

Dwarf Alberta Spruce
Picea glauca var. *albertiana* 'Conica'
Evergreen shrub; 10–12'; fine, dense, light green leaves; conical form; sun to part shade; zones 2–6; *p. 216*

Dwarf Baby's Breath
Gypsophila paniculata 'Compacta Plena'
Perennial; 18"; summer; white; sun; zones 3–7; *p. 71*

Dwarf Blue Fescue

Festuca glauca 'Nana'
Perennial; 6–10"; silvery blue leaves; sun to light shade; zones 4–8; *pp. 79, 204*

Dwarf Cattail
Typha minima
Aquatic perennial; to 30"; summer to fall; dark brown; sun or part shade; zones 3–10; *p. 173*

Dwarf Creeping Indigo
Indigofera pseudotinctoria
Subshrub; 4–6'; summer to fall; pale red, pink, white; sun; zones 6–9; *p. 53*

Dwarf Lavender Cotton
Santolina chamaecyparissus 'Nana'
Perennial herb; 6"; summer; bright yellow; silvery evergreen leaves; sun; zones 6–9; *p. 163*

E

Echeveria
Evergreen succulent perennial; 4–12"; rosettes of leaves in various colors; sun; zones 8–10; *p. 156*
• *E. setosa*: 1–3'; late spring to summer; yellow tipped red; rosettes of leaves covered with white hairs; *p. 148*

Echinopsis
Perennial cactus; 3–6'; summer; yellow, red, white; sun; zones 9–10; *p. 157*

Edging Lobelia 'Paper Moon'
Lobelia erinus 'Paper Moon'
Annual; 4–6"; summer to fall; white; part shade or sun; *p. 41*

Elecampane
Inula helenium
Perennial; 4–7'; summer; yellow; sun to light shade; zones 3–8; *p. 85*

Elderberry 'Sutherland Gold'

annual; 12–24"; spring to summer; white, various pastels; sun; zones 9–10; *pp. 69, 121*

French Lavender
Lavandula stoechas
Evergreen shrub; 2'; late spring to summer; dark purple; edible flowers; aromatic flowers and leaves; sun; zones 7–9; *pp. 119, 163, 226*

French Marigold
Tagetes patula
Annual; 6–18"; summer to frost; yellow, orange, red, bicolors; sun; *p. 34*

Fringed Bleeding Heart
Dicentra eximia
Perennial; 9–18"; spring to summer; rose pink; sun or part shade; zones 3–9; *p. 67*

G

Garden Forget-Me-Not
Myosotis sylvatica
Biennial; 9–24"; spring; blue; part shade; zones 3–7; *pp. 123, 125*

Garden Phlox
Phlox paniculata
Perennial; 3–4'; summer; white, pink, purple, red; fragrant; sun to part shade; zones 4–8; *pp. 81, 220*
- 'Blue Paradise': 24–36"; lavender blue; *p. 68*
- 'Bright Eyes': pale pink with crimson eye; *pp. 86, 126*
- 'Orange Perfection': 2'; deep orange; *p. 28*

Garden Pinks
Dianthus plumarius cvs.
Perennial; 8–24"; early summer; pink, rose, white, single or double; edible flowers; fragrant; gray green evergreen leaves; sun, part shade; zones 3–8; *p. 112*

Garland Flower
Daphne cneorum
Evergreen shrub; 8–12"; spring; pink, extremely fragrant; part shade; zones 5–7; *pp. 121, 210*

Garlic
Allium sativum
Bulb; 24"; spring to summer; white to pink; edible; sun to part shade; *p. 182*

Garlic Chives
Allium tuberosum
Perennial herb; 10–20"; late summer to fall; white; edible flowers; sun to light shade; zones 4–8; *p. 81*

Gas Plant
Dictamnus albus 'Purpureus'
Perennial; 3–4'; early summer; mauve; sun; zones 3–7; *p. 208*

Geranium
Pelargonium × hortorum
Evergreen perennial; 1–2'; spring to fall; white, pink, red, purple; sun; zones 7–10.
- 'Pink Elite': 6"; pink; *p. 80*
- 'Pinto Red': deep red; *p. 99*

Geranium (Cranesbill)
Perennial; 6–36"; late spring to early fall; white to purple; sun to part shade; zones 3–10 *pp. 57, 223*
- 'Brookside': 12–24"; summer to fall; violetblue; *p. 122*
- *G. cinereum subcaulescens*: 6–12"; spring; magenta with black centers; zones 5–7; *p. 112*
- *G. ibericum*: 18–24"; violet blue; *p. 192*
- 'Johnson's Blue' (*G.* Johnson's Blue'): 15–18"; all summer; blue violet; zones 4–7; *pp. 46, 48, 49, 106*
- 'Wargrave Pink' (*G. endressii* 'Wargrave Pink'): 15–18"; summer; pink; zones 4–7; *p. 62*

Geum

Perennial; 20–24"; spring; yellow, orange, red; sun to light shade; zones 4–7; *p. 206*
- 'Mrs. J. Bradshaw': scarlet; *pp. 108, 172*

Giant Allium
Allium giganteum
Bulb; 5'; summer; lilac pink; sun to part shade; zones 6–10; *p. 235*

Giant Chain Fern
Woodwardia fimbriata
Deciduous fern; 3'; green, lance-shaped fronds; part shade; zones 8–9; *p. 196*

Giant Wild Parsnip
Angelica gigas
Perennial; 3–5'; late summer to fall; deep purple; sun to part shade; zones 5–7; *p. 93*

Ginger Mint
Mentha × gracilis
Perennial; 12"; summer; lilac; edible flowers; red-tinted stems; leaves aromatic and ginger flavored; sun to part shade; zones 6–9; *p. 186*

Gladiola
Gladiolus cvs.
Bulb; 2–4'; summer; various colors; sun; zones 8–10; *p. 177*
- 'Violetta': Butterfly type; 4–5'; violet with white streaks; *p. 65*
- 'Pallas': 3–4'; pink with white throat; *p. 52*

Globe Amaranth
Gomphrena globosa
Annual; 8–24"; summer to fall; pink, purple, red, white; everlasting flowers; sun; *pp. 202, 210*
- 'Strawberry Fields': 2'; red; *p. 141*

Globeflower 'Orange Princess'
Trollius × cultorum 'Orange Princess'
Perennial; 2'; late spring; deep orange; sun to part shade; zones 3–6; *p. 94*

shell pink; part to full shade or sun; zones 5–8; *p. 217*

Hibiscus
Hibiscus moscheutos
Perennial; 4–8'; summer to frost; pink, rose, white; edible flowers; sun, part shade; zones 5–9.
• 'Disco Belle Hybrids': 20"; compact strain, often grown as an annual; *p. 85*
• 'Southern Belle Hybrids': to 4'; red, pink, white; *p. 200*

Hibiscus 'Red Shield'
Hibiscus acetosella 'Red Shield'
Annual; 2–5'; late summer to fall; purple red, yellow; edible flowers; maroon leaves; sun; *p. 174*

Hollyhock 'The Watchman Strain'
Alcea rosea 'The Watchman Strain'
Perennial; 3–5'; summer to fall; sun; dark maroon; edible flowers; zones 3–7; *p. 54*

Hollyhock Mallow
Malva alcea
Perennial; 2–4'; summer to fall; purplish pink, white; sun or part shade; zones 4–7; *pp. 63, 103*

Honeysuckle 'John Clayton'
Lonicera sempervirens 'John Clayton'
Perennial vine; 10–20'; spring to fall; golden yellow; sun or part shade; zones 4–9; *p. 174*

Hoop Petticoat Daffodil
Narcissus bulbocodium
Bulb; 8–12"; midspring; yellow, funnel shaped; sun to part shade; zones 3–9; *p. 105*

Hosta
Perennial; 6–36"; summer; white, lavender, purple flowers, some fragrant; various leaves colors and variegations; zones 3–8; light to deep shade; *p. 204*
• 'Albomarginata' (*H. undulata* var. *albomarginata*): 12", 36" in flower;

purple; green leaves with white margins; *pp. 142, 147, 208*
• 'Elegans' (*H. sieboldiana elegans*): 3'; lilac; gray blue leaves; *p. 49*
• 'Frances Williams' (*H. s.* 'Frances Williams'): 2–3'; white; blue green leaves with chartreuse margins; *pp. 208, 219*
• 'Gold Standard': 26"; lilac; green yellow leaves with irregular dark green margins; *p. 223*
• *H. crispula*: 8–12"; lavender; green leaves with white margin; *p. 43*
• *H. montana*: 30"; white; green, heavily veined leaves; *p. 40*
• 'Lovepat': 18"; off white; cupped, puckered, glaucous, blue green leaves; *p. 232*
• 'Mediovariegata' (*H. undulata* 'Mediovariegata'): 3'; mauve; twisted leaves with central white markings; *p. 186*
• 'Northern Exposure': 3'; white; blue green leaves with yellow green margins; *p. 180*
• 'Northern Halo': 20"; white; blue green leaves edged cream; *p. 43*
• 'Patriot': 12–18"; pale lilac; green leaves widely edged white; *p. 145*
• 'Paul's Glory': 1–2'; lavender; yellow leaves with green edges; *p. 115*
• 'Piedmont Gold': 20"; grayish white; wavy margined, glaucous, yellow green leaves; *p. 232*
• 'Sharmon' (*H. fortunei* 'Sharmon'): 20–24"; late summer; lavender; greenish yellow leaves with dark green, wavy margins; *p. 115*
• 'Sun Power': 24"; lavender to white; yellow, wavy leaves; *p. 38*
• 'Twilight': 22"; lavender; dark green with wide yellow margins; *p. 115*

Hyacinth 'Pink Perfection'
Hyacinthus orientalis 'Pink Perfection'
Bulb; 8–12"; spring; medium pink; sun to light shade; zones 4–7; *p. 87*

Hydrangea 'Tardiva'

Hydrangea paniculata 'Tardiva'
Deciduous shrub; 15–25'; fall; creamy white, aging to pink; part shade or sun; zones 3–8; *p. 200*

Iceland Poppy
Papaver nudicaule
Perennial; 12–18"; spring; white, yellow, red, pastels; sun; zones 2–7; *p. 182*

Ice Plant
Dorotheanthus bellidiformus
Annual; 4–6"; summer; various colors; full sun; *p. 115*

Impatiens 'Fiesta Pink'
Impatiens walleriana 'Fiesta Pink'
Perennial, usually grown as an annual; 12–24"; summer to frost; double pink; light to deep shade; Zone 10; *p. 50*

Indian Fig
Opuntia ficus-indica
Cactus; 15'; late spring and summer; yellow flowers, followed by edible purple fruit; sun; zones 9–10; *p. 213*

Irish Moss
Minuartia verna (*Arenaria verna*)
Perennial; 1–3", spreading; summer; white; part shade, sun; zones 2–7; *pp. 139, 209*

Italian Arum
Arum italicum 'Pictum'
Perennial; 18"; spring; creamy white; orange berries in fall; green leaves with gray and cream markings; part to full shade; zones 6–9; *p. 142*

Ixote
Yucca elephantipes
Evergreen shrub; to 30'; summer to fall; creamy white; sun; zones 10–11; *p. 213*

J

Jack-in-the-Pulpit
Arisaema sikokianum
Perennial; 12–20"; early spring; striped purple brown and white; part shade; zones 5–8; *p. 189*

Japanese Anemone
Anemone × hybrida
Perennial; 3–4'; late summer to early fall; white to deep pink; sun or part shade; zones 5–10; *p. 45*

Japanese Barberry
Berberis thunbergii;
Deciduous shrub; 2–3'; leaves colors (red, yellow, green, variegated); sun to part shade; zones 4–8; *pp. 93, 166*

Japanese Blood Grass
Imperata cylindrica 'Red Baron'
Perennial; 12–18"; red leaves; sun; zones 6–9; *pp. 71, 140, 223, 225*

Japanese Butterbur
Petasites japonicus
Perennial; 3'; late winter to early spring; yellowish white; large, kidney shaped leaves; part to full shade; zones 5–9; *p. 219*

Japanese Cutleaf Maple
Acer palmatum dissectum 'Atropurpureum'
Deciduous tree; 5–12'; fernlike, deep red leaves, turning orange in fall; twisted branching pattern; sun to part shade; zones 6–8; *pp. 213, 219*

Japanese Euonymus 'Silver Knight'
Euonymus japonicus 'Silver Knight'
Evergreen shrub; 3–12'; leaves glossy green with white margins; sun to part shade; zones 6–9; *p. 45*

Japanese Ginger
Asarum splendens
Perennial; 12–15"; leaves dark green with silver bands; shade; zones 6–8; *p. 180*

Japanese Holly 'Convexa'
Ilex crenata 'Convexa'
Evergreen shrub; to 8'; purple green stems with curling, glossy, dark green leaves; black fruits; sun to part shade; zones 5–7; *p. 230*

Japanese Iris
Iris ensata
Perennial; 24–30"; summer; white, pink, blue, purple; sun or part shade; zones 4–9; *pp. 99, 102*
• 'Henry's White': 36"; white; *p. 79*

Japanese Maple
Acer palmatum
Deciduous tree; 5–25'; delicate leaves in shades of green, red, or purple; sun to part shade; zones 6–8; *pp. 149, 213*

Japanese Painted Fern
Athyrium nipponicum 'Pictum'
Perennial; 12–18"; silver, pink, green variegated leaves; shade; zones 3–8; *pp. 45, 67, 180, 204, 205*

Japanese Photinia
Photinia glabra
Evergreen shrub; 10–12'; early summer; white, followed by red fruit aging to black; leaves red when young; sun to part shade; zones 7–9; *p. 191*

Japanese Primrose
Primula japonica
Perennial; 18"; spring; red purple to white; part shade; zones 3–8; *p. 78*

Japanese Rose
Kerria japonica
Deciduous shrub; 4–6'; late spring; golden yellow, single or double; sun to part shade; zones 4–9; *p. 230*

Japanese Shield Fern (Autumn Fern)

Dryopteris erythrosora
Evergreen perennial; 24"; young leaves copper red, turning dark green; part shade; zones 6–9; *p. 204*

Japanese Sweet Flag
Acorus gramineus 'Variegatus'
Perennial; 12"; leaves green with cream stripes; part shade to full sun; zones 5–8; *p. 38*

Japanese Wavy-Leaved Hosta
Hosta undulata var. *albomarginata*
Perennial; 12–18"; summer; purple; green leaves with wavy white margins; shade; zones 3–8; *pp. 44, 210*

Japanese Wild Ginger
Asarum asaroides
Evergreen perennial; 8"; leaves with cloudy silver markings; part shade; zones 6–9; *pp. 45, 221*

Joe-Pye Weed
Eupatorium purpureum
Perennial; 6–8'; late summer to fall; pink; sun to part shade; zones 3–8; *p. 226*

Jointed Rush
Juncus articulatus
Perennial; 2–3'; summer to fall; brown; grasslike cylindrical stems; grow in wet areas; sun or part shade; zones 5–8; *pp. 173, 219*

Jonquil
Narcissus jonquilla
Bulb; 12"; spring; golden yellow; fragrant; sun to part shade; zones 5–9; *p. 172*

Joseph's Coat
Alternanthera ficoidea
Annual; 6–12"; leaves with various colors and variegations; sun; *p. 147*
• 'Versicolor': 12"; spoon-shaped, copper to maroon leaves; *p. 234*

Juniper
Juniperus spp.
Evergreen shrub, upright or

spreading; 5–50'; fine, scaley leaves; sun; zones 3–9; *pp. 149, 205*
• 'Depressa 'Aurea' (*J. communis* 'Depressa Aurea'): Evergreen shrub; 2'; golden yellow foliage, turning bronze, then green over winter; sun or part shade; zones 3–7; *pp. 149, 194, 216, 219*

Jupiter's Beard
Centranthus ruber
Perennial; 18–36"; rose pink; sun to part shade; zones 4–10; *pp. 61, 81, 86, 103, 159, 220*

K

Kaffir Lily
Schizostylis coccinea
Perennial; to 24"; fall; scarlet; sun; zones 7–9; *pp. 200, 203*

Kale
Brassica oleracea Acephala group
Annual vegetable; 10–24"; spring, fall; crisp, often curly leaves, green, red, purple; sun.
• 'Blond': heirloom variety; pale chartreuse ruffled leaves; *p. 110*
• 'Lacinato': heirloom variety; thick, crinkled blue green leaves; *p. 163*
• 'Purple': heirloom variety; deep burgundy ruffled leaves; *p. 110*
• 'Redbor': ruffled blue green leaves with purple veins; *p. 163*
• 'Winterbor': 36"; frilly, deep blue green leaves; *p. 182*

Kamtschatka Sedum
Sedum kamtschaticum
Perennial; 12"; summer; yellow, turning crimson; sun to part shade; zones 3–8; *pp. 121, 139*

Keeled Garlic
Allium carinatum subsp. *pulchellum*
Bulb; perennial; 12–18"; summer; purple; evergreen leaves; sun to part shade; zones 6–9; *p. 113*

Knap Hill Hybrid Azalea
Rhododendron Knap Hill Hybrid
Deciduous shrub; 4–9'; late spring;
pink, cream, yellow, orange, red;
fragrant; full to part shade; zones
5–7; *p. 185*

Knautia
Knautia macedonica
Perennial; 2–3'; summer; deep
maroon; sun; zones 4–9; *p. 70*

Knotweed 'Magic Carpet'
Polygonum capitatum 'Magic
Carpet'
Perennial; 3"; summer; pink; sun,
part shade; zones 8–9; *p. 67*

Korean Azalea
Rhododendron mucronulatum
Deciduous shrub; 4–8'; midspring;
rosy purple; full to part shade; zones
4–7; *p. 100*

L

Lacecap Hydrangea 'Blue Wave'
Hydrangea macrophylla 'Blue Wave'
Deciduous shrub; 6–7'; mid- to late
summer; rich blue to mauve; sun to
part shade; zones 6–9; *p. 152*

Lady Banks Rose (Banksia Rose)
Rosa banksiae var. *normalis* 'Lutea'
Deciduous climber; 20'; late spring,
yellow; sun to part shade; zones
8–9; *pp. 63, 230*

Ladybells
Adenophora confusa
Perennial; 24–30"; late spring; blue,
lilac; sun or part shade; zones 3–7;
p. 85

Lady's Mantle
Alchemilla mollis
Perennial; 1–2'; late spring to early
summer; chartreuse; shade; zones
3–9; *pp. 82, 101, 113, 142, 208*
• 'Thriller': 18"; flowers more fluffy

and numerous; *p. 33*

Lamb's Ears
Stachys byzantina
Perennial; 12–18"; spring; purple,
pink; velvety silver leaves; sun, light
shade; zones 4–10; *pp. 67, 76,
112, 114, 146, 159, 206, 235*

Lance Coreopsis 'Baby Sun'
Coreopsis lanceolata 'Baby Sun'
Perennial; 1–2'; late spring; yellow;
sun; zones 3–8; *p. 33*

Lantana
Lantana camara cultivars
Shrub, often grown as an annual;
3–6'; spring to late fall; various
colors; sun; Zone 10; *pp. 29, 183*
• 'Miss Huff's Hardy': 36"; orange
and pink; hardy to Zone 7; *p. 202*

Large Blue Fescue
Festuca amethystina
Perennial; 18"; late spring to early
summer; violet tinted green;
threadlike, silvery, blue green leaves;
sun; zones 4–8; *p. 228*

Larkspur
Consolida ambigua
Annual; 1–4'; summer; white, pink,
blue, purple; sun or light shade;
pp. 72, 74
• 'Eastern Blues': 2–3'; deep blue;
p. 116

Lavatera 'Eye Catcher'
Perennial; 4–5'; summer; deep rose
with red veins and centers; sun;
zones 5–10; *p. 52*

Lavatera 'Silver Cup'
Lavatera trimestris 'Silver Cup'
Annual; 30"; summer; glowing pink
with darker veining; sun; *p. 192*

Lavender Cotton
Santolina chamaecyparissus
Perennial herb; 1–2'; summer;
bright yellow; grayish evergreen
leaves; sun; zones 6–9; *pp. 46,
160, 179*

Leatherleaf Sedge
Carex buchananii
Perennial sedge; 15–18"; leaves
coppery red to bronze; sun to
part shade; zones 7–9; *pp. 139,
166, 223*

Leek
Allium porrum
Biennial grown as annual vegetable;
2'; 100 to 105 days; blue leaves;
sun; *pp. 182, 213*
• 'Blue Solaise': 2'; blue leaves turn
violet in cool weather; *p. 203*

Lemon Daylily
Hemerocallis lilioasphodelus
(*H. citrina*)
Perennial; 4'; summer; pale yellow;
edible flowers; fragrant; sun to part
shade; zones 3–10; *p. 170*

Lemon Thyme
Thymus × citriodorus
Perennial herb; to 12"; summer;
lavender pink; edible flowers;
lemon-scented leaves; sun; zones
6–9; *pp. 164, 235*

Lenten Rose
Helleborus orientalis
Evergreen perennial; 15–18"; early
spring; white to purple; part shade;
zones 4–9; *pp. 51, 178*

Leopard's Bane
Doronicum orientale
Perennial; 1–2'; spring; yellow; sun
to part shade; zones 4–7; *pp. 121,
176*

Lesser Celandine
Ranunculus ficaria
Perennial; 2"; early spring; yellow,
fading to white; invasive; part to full
shade; zones 4–8; *p. 33*

Lettuce
Lactuca sativa
Annual; 6–12"; 45 to 60 days;
spring to fall harvest; green or red
leaves; sun.
• 'Brunia': red bronze, oakleaf; *p. 78*

evergreen
shrubs for
four seasons

Azalea
Big Leaf Wintercreeper
Bloodleaf Banana
Boxwood 'Kingsville Dwarf'
Chinese Holly
Cliff--Green
English Lavender
Japanese Euonymus 'Silver Knight'
Japanese Holly 'Convexa'
Japanese Photinia
London Pride
Mexican Bush Sage
Pork and Beans
Rhododendron
Rock Rose
Rosemary
Skeleton Rose Geranium
Scotch Heather
Sheep Laurel 'Rubra'
Sotol
Variegated Myrtle
Variegated Pittosporum
Variegated Wintercreeper

texture from
needled
evergreens

Blue Spruce
Canadian Hemlock
Chamaecyparis
Chinese Spruce
Colorado Blue Spruce
Dwarf Alberta Spruce
False Cypress 'Nana Aurea'
Gold Juniper
Golden Sawara Cypress
Junipers
Oriental Arborvitae
Russian Cypress
Weeping Serbian Spruce

Oxeye Daisy (Common Daisy)
Leucanthemum vulgare
Perennial; 1–3'; summer; white with yellow centers; sun to part shade; zones 3–10; *pp. 83, 226*

Pachysandra 'Silver Edge'
Pachysandra terminalis 'Silver Edge'
Evergreen perennial; 9–12"; spring; creamy white; leaves green variegated with white; part shade; zones 4–9; *p. 176*

Painted Daisy (Pyrethrum)
Tanacetum coccineum
Perennial; 1–2'; early summer; red, pink, white; sun, part shade; zones 3–7; *pp. 114, 115, 120, 226*

Pampas Grass
Cortaderia selloana
Perennial; 4–7'; summer; silver to cream plumes; sun to part shade; zones 6–9; *pp. 174, 231*
• Sun Stripe™: leaves yellow with green margins; *pp. 166, 223*

Pansy
Viola × wittrockiana hybrids
Perennial grown as an annual; 6–9"; spring, fall (winter in cool regions); mixed colors; part shade; zones 4–8; *pp. 78, 126*
• 'Giant White': large white; *p. 41*

Papyrus
Cyperus papyrus
Perennial; to 6'; umbrellalike cluster of tiny brown flowers; sun to part shade; zones 9–10; *p. 219*

Pasqueflower
Pulsatilla vulgaris (Anemone pulsatilla)
Perennial; 9–12"; early spring; purple; furry leaves; sun; zones 5–7; *p. 78*

Pennyroyal
Mentha pulegium
Perennial herb; 4–12"; summer; pink, lilac; fragrant leaves; sun to part shade; zones 7–9; *p. 147*

Penstemon 'Husker Red'
Penstemon digitalis 'Husker Red'
Perennial; 2–3'; summer; white flowers; maroon leaves; sun or part shade; zones 4–8; *pp. 79, 139*

Peony
Paeonia spp.
Perennial; 2–3'; spring; white, pink, red, yellow; sun; zones 2–10.
• 'Kansas': 3'; double red; fragrant; *p. 121*
• 'Sarah Bernhardt': 3'; double rose pink; fragrant; *p. 51*

Perennial Fountain Grass
Pennisetum alopecuroides 'Hameln'
Perennial; 24–30"; late summer to fall; silvery white; sun to part shade; zones 5–9; *pp. 168, 232*

Perennial Sunflower
Helianthus × multiflorus
Perennial; 3–5'; late summer to fall; golden yellow; sun; zones 4–8; *p. 35*

Periwinkle
Vinca minor
Perennial groundcover; 6"; spring; lavender purple; sun, shade; zones 4–7; *pp. 45, 82, 101*

Perky Sue
Tetraneuris scaposa
Perennial; 6–9"; bright yellow; native to SW US; sun; zones 4–7; *p. 150*

Persian Buttercup
Ranunculus asiaticus
Bulb; 12–18"; spring; many colors; sun to part shade; zones 8–10; *p. 110*

Persian Onion
Allium aflatunense
Bulb; 2–3'; late spring; pinkish purple; sun or part shade; zones 4–8; *p. 194*

Persian Shield
Strobilanthes dyerianus
Deciduous shrub; 2–4'; purple flushed green leaves; sun or part shade; zone 10; *p. 136*

Peruvian Daffodil
Hymenocallis spp.
Bulb; 2'; summer; white; very fragrant; sun or part shade; zones 8–11; *p. 188*

Petunia
Petunia × hybrida
Annual; 8–18"; late spring to fall; various colors; sun, light shade; *pp. 41, 52*
• 'Purple Wave': 6" tall, up to 4' spread; magenta purple; *p. 121*
• 'White Magic': 9"; large white flowers, compact plant; *p. 63*

Phlox 'Phlox of Sheep'
Phlox drummondii 'Phlox of Sheep'
Annual; 10–12"; summer; various pastels; sun to part shade; *p. 61*

Pincushion Flower
Scabiosa columbaria
Perennial; 1–2'; summer; blue, lavender, white; sun to light shade; zones 3–8; *p. 100*
• Butterfly Blue™: 16"; lavender blue; *p. 125*
• 'Pink Mist': 16"; lavender pink; *p. 84*

Pink Cardinal Flower
Lobelia cardinalis
Perennial; 2–4'; summer to fall; shades of pink; full sun to part shade; zones 2–9; *p. 108*

Pinks 'Brilliancy'
Dianthus 'Brilliancy'
Perennial; 6"; early summer; vivid red; sun; zones 3–8; *p. 125*

Pinwheel
Aeonium haworthii

sweeten the bed with
fragrant
flowers

Abyssian Gladiolus
Angel's Trumpet
Burkwood Viburnum
Calamondin Tree
Butterfly Bush
Chaste Tree
Cheddar Pinks
Chilean Jasmine
Cottage Pinks
Dame's Rocket
Daphne
Datura
Dianthus
English Lavender
Exbury Hybrid Azalea
Flowering Tobacco
Freesia
Garden Phlox
Garden Pinks
Garland Flower
Heliotrope
Hosta
Hyacinth 'Pink Perfection'
Japanese Wavy-Leafed Hosta
Jonquil
Knap Hill Azalea
Lemon Daylily
Lemon Thyme
Lily
Lily-of-the-Valley
Meyer Lemon
Maiden Pinks
Peony
Petunia
Pinks 'Brilliancy'
Prairie Dropseed
Regal Lily
Rose
Rosemary
Silver-Edged Lemon Thyme
Stock
Summer Hyacinth
Sweet Alyssum
Sweet Autumn Clematis
Sweet Pea 'Vibrant Firecrest'
Sweet Violet
Sweet Woodruff
Variegated Pittosporum
Virginia Sweetspire 'Henry's Garnet'

zones 5–8; *p. 84*

Redleaf Rose
Rosa glauca (R. rubrifolia)
Deciduous shrub; 6'; spring; single, cerise pink; reddish stems, purplish gray leaves; sun to part shade; zones 2–8; *p. 163*

Red Orach
Atriplex hortensis var. rubra
Annual; 3–4'; summer; blood red leaves and flowers; sun; *p. 78*

Red Sorrel
Rumex acetosa
Perennial; 4–8"; summer; red-flecked green leaves; shade or sun; zones 6–8; *p. 110*

Regal Lily
Lilium regale
Bulb; 4–6'; summer; white; fragrant; part shade, sun; zones 3–9; *p. 102*

Rhododendron
Evergreen shrub; 3–15'; spring; white, pink, lavender; part shade, sun; zones 4–8, depending on species; *p. 221*
• 'P.J.M.': 3–6'; lavender pink; zones 5–8; *pp. 109, 196*

Rhubarb 'Valentine'
Rheum × cultorum 'Valentine'
Perennial; 2–4'; edible, deep red stalks; sun to part shade; zones 3–9; *p. 200*

Ribbon Grass
Phalaris arundinacea
Perennial; 18–24"; green leaves with white stripes; sun, shade; zones 4–9; *pp. 79, 139*

Rock Anise Hyssop
Agastache rupestris
Perennial; 3–4'; summer; rosy orange; licorice-scented leaves; sun; zones 5–8; *p. 213*

Rock Rose

Cistus incanus ssp. *creticus*
Evergreen shrub; 24–30"; summer; mauve pink; sun; zones 8–9; *p. 53*

Rockspray Cotoneaster
Cotoneaster horizontalis
Decidous shrub; 3'; late spring; pinkish white flowers; red fruit summer to fall; sun; zones 5–7; *pp. 26, 157, 166*

Rocky Mountain Columbine
Aquilegia caerulea
Perennial; 1–2'; spring; blue and white; sun, part shade; zones 3–8; *p. 48*

Rodgersia 'Rosea'
Rodgersia pinnata 'Rosea'
Perennial; 3–4'; late spring; rose red; part shade or sun; zones 5–7; *p. 141*

Romaine Lettuce 'Olga'
Lactuca sativa 'Olga'
Annual vegetable; 8"; 50 days; uniform, light green heads; sun to part shade; *p. 150*

Rose
Rosa spp. and hybrids
Deciduous shrub; 1–12'; late spring to frost; various colors; fragrant; sun, part shade; zones 2–10, depending on species.
• Abraham Darby™: Shrub; 5'; apricot pink double; *p. 28*
• 'Betty Prior': Floribunda; 2–4'; hot pink, single, nonstop bloom; *p. 80*
• Brandy™: Hybrid tea; golden apricot flowers, red-tinted leaves; *p. 84*
• 'Europeana': Floribunda; 2–4'; dark crimson; *p. 123*
• 'Flower Carpet Red': groundcover; 20–30"; red flowers; *p. 197*
• 'La Belle Sultane' ('Violacea'): Gallica; 7'; single violet purple; fragrant; *p. 56*
• 'Louise Odier': Bourbon; 6'; early summer and fall; double pink; fragrant; *p. 215*
• 'Sparrieshoop': 5'; single pink;

zones 4–8; *p. 65*

Rose Campion
Lychnis coronaria
Perennial; 18–36"; summer; magenta; silver leaves; sun; zones 3–10; *pp. 72, 78, 194, 229*

Rosemary
Rosemararinus officinalis
Evergreen shrub; 2–6'; summer; blue; edible flowers; aromatic leaves; sun; zones 7–10; *p. 113*

Rose Periwinkle
Catharanthus roseus
Evergreen perennial, usually grown as an annual; 1–2'; spring through summer; white, pink, rose, red; sun to part shade; Zone 10; *p. 223*

Rose Scented Geranium
Pelargonium graveolens 'Rober's Lemon Rose'
Evergreen perennial; 18–24"; spring to fall; mauve; edible flowers; rose/lemon-scented, finely cut leaves; sun to part shade; zones 10–11; *p. 67*

Royal Fern
Osmunda regalis
Perennial fern; 4–6'; bright green fronds; part shade or sun; zones 4–9; *p. 181*

Rudbeckia (Black-Eyed Susan) 'Goldsturm'
Rudbeckia fulgida var. sullivantii 'Goldsturm'
Perennial; 18–24"; summer to fall; yellow gold with dark centers; sun to part shade; zones 3–10; *pp. 104, 194, 226*

Rue
Ruta graveolens
Evergreen subshrub; 1–3'; summer; pale yellow; blue green, aromatic leaves; sun; zones 4–8; *p. 220*

Russian Cypress
Microbiota decussata

3–7; *pp. 93, 152*

Siberian Bugloss
Brunnera macrophylla
Perennial; 12–18"; spring; blue; shade; zones 3–7; *pp. 82, 123*

Siberian Catmint
Nepeta sibirica
Perennial; 24–36"; summer; lavender; zones 3–7; full sun to part shade; *pp. 65, 137*

Siberian Iris
Iris sibirica
Perennial; 24–48"; late spring, early summer; white to purple; sun, part shade; zones 4–10; *pp. 106, 108*

Siberian Squill
Scilla siberica
Bulb, 4–8"; early spring; deep blue; zones 4–8; full sun or part shade; *p. 105*

Siberian Tea
Bergenia crassifolia
Perennial; 18"; late winter to early spring; pinkish purple flowers; reddish green stems; part shade; zones 4–8; *p. 232*

Silver and Gold
Dendranthema pacificum
Perennial; 1–2'; late fall; yellow; silver-edged leaves; sun; zones 5–9; *pp. 44, 176*

Silver-Edged Lemon Thyme
Thymus × citriodorus 'Argenteus'
Perennial herb; to 12"; summer; lavender pink; edible flowers; silver-edged, lemon-scented leaves; sun; zones 6–9; *p. 186*

Silver Sage
Salvia argentea
Perennial; 2–4'; large, wooly silver white leaves; sun; zones 6–8; *p. 220*

Skeleton Rose Geranium
Pelargonium radens 'Dr. Livingstone'

Evergreen subshrub; 2–4'; spring to summer; purple pink; edible flowers; aromatic gray green leaves; sun or part shade; zones 8–10; *p. 174*

Smooth Hydrangea
Hydrangea arborescens
Deciduous shrub; 3–5'; summer; white; sun or part shade; zones 4–9; *p. 43*
• 'Annabelle': white flowers up to 12" across; superior form; *p. 160*

Snapdragon
Antirrhinum majus
Annual; 6–48"; early summer to fall; various colors; sun to part shade; *p. 126*
• 'Jamaican Mist': 12"; various warm and pastel shades; *p. 61*

Sneezewort 'The Pearl'
Achillea ptarmica 'The Pearl'
Perennial; 18–24"; summer; creamy white; sun to part shade; zones 2–9; *pp. 179, 225*

Snow Crocus
Crocus tommasinianus
Bulb; 3–4"; late winter to spring; silvery lilac to reddish purple; sun; zones 3–8; *p. 51*

Snow-in-Summer
Cerastium tomentosum
Perennial; 6–12"; spring; white flowers; silver leaves; sun; zones 3–10; *pp. 60, 74, 112, 139, 148*

Snow-on-the-Mountain
Euphorbia marginata
Annual; 2–4'; summer to frost; silvery green and white variegated leaves; sun or part shade; *p. 171*

Sotol
Dasylirion texanum 'Glaucum'
Evergreen shrub; to 15'; early summer; white; glaucous leaves; sun; zones 9–10; *p. 223*

Spanish Bluebell
Hyacinthoides hispanica (Scilla

campanulata)
Bulb; 16"; spring; blue, white, pink; part shade or sun; zones 4–9; *pp. 67, 87, 180, 183*

Spider Flower 'Pink Queen'
Cleome hassleriana 'Pink Queen'
Annual; 3–4'; summer to fall; pink; sun, part shade; *pp. 120, 126*

Spiderwort
Tradescantia virginiana
Perennial; 18–36"; late spring to fall; white to blue; sun or part shade; zones 4–10; *p. 78*
• *T* x *andersoniana* 'Zwanenburg Blue'; 20–24"; deep royal blue; *p. 49*

Spiny Bear's Breeches
Acanthus spinosus
Perennial; 3–4'; late spring; purple and white; large spiny leaves; sun or part shade; zones 6–10; *p. 163*

Spirea
Spiraea japonica
Deciduous shrub; 2–6'; summer; white to deep pink flowers; green or gold leaves; sun or part shade; zones 4–8.
• 'Gold Flame': 30"; dark pink flowers; gold leaves, aging to orange; *p. 191*
• 'Gold Mound': 30–42"; pink flowers; yellow leaves, aging to yellow green; *p. 147*

Spotted Dead Nettle
Lamium maculatum
Perennial; 8–12"; spreading; spring to early summer; pink to purple; leaves with white or silver markings; part shade; zones 3–8; *p. 67*

Spotted Lungwort
Pulmonaria saccharata
Perennial; 8–18"; spring; opening pink, turning blue; leaves with silver spots; part shade, adequate moisture; zones 3–9; *p. 45*

Spring Starflower

Hosta
Italian Arum
Japanese Euonymus 'Silver Knight'
Japanese Ginger
Japanese Painted Fern
Japanese Shield Fern
Japanese Sweet Flag
Japanese Wavy Leafed Hosta
Japanese Wild Ginger
Long-Leafed Lungwort
Lungwort
Maiden Grass
Manna Grass
Pachysandra 'Silver Edge'
Plectranthus
Porcupine Grass
Ribbon Grass
Silver and Gold
Silver-Edged Lemon Thyme
Snow-on-the-Mountain
Spotted Dead Nettle
Spotted Lungwort
Strawberry Geranium
Variegated Bulbous Oat Grass
Variegated Busy-Lizzy
Variegated Forsters Plectranthus
Variegated Giant Reed
Variegated Goutweed
Variegated Japanese Hops
Variegated Japanese Sedge
Variegated Licorice Plant
Variegated Lily-of-the-Valley
Variegated Money Plant
Variegated Myrtle
Variegated Pachysandra
Variegated Pittosporum
Variegated Porcelain Berry
Variegated Purple Moor Grass
Variegated Red Twig Dogwood
Variegated Siberian Bugloss
Variegated Society Garlic
Variegated St. John's Wort
Variegated Velvet Grass
Variegated Viola
Variegated Wintercreeper
Yellow Archangel 'Herman's Pride'

deep shade; zones 4–8; *p. 235*

Tomato 'Angora'
Lycopersicon esculentum 'Angora'
Annual vegetable; 68 days; grayish
white fuzzy leaves; brilliant red fruits;
indeterminate; sun; *p. 213*

Toothed Wood Fern
Dryopteris carthusiana
Perennial; to 24"; delicate
pale green fronds; part shade;
zones 5–8; *p. 207*

Torch Plant
Aloe aristata
Succulent perennial; to 5"; fall;
orange red; evergreen dark green
leaves with white spots and spines;
sun; zones 9–10; *p. 228*

Tovara 'Painter's Palette'
Polygonum virginianum 'Painter's
Palette'
Perennial; 2–4', spreading to 6'; late
summer to fall; pink; leaves
variegated green with gold and pink
brown; part shade; zones 5–8;
pp. 39, 70

Tradescantia 'Purple Heart'
Tradescantia pallida 'Purple Heart'
Trailing perennial; 8"; summer, pink;
violet purple leaves; sun to part
shade; zones 8–10; *pp. 54, 55,
147*

Tree Mallow
Lavatera trimestris
Annual; 2–4'; summer; pink, rose,
white; sun; *p. 117*

Tricolor Corn
Zea mays 'Harlequin'
Annual vegetable; 4–6'; leaves
striped green, red, and white; dark
red ears; sun; *p. 213*

Triplet Lily
Triteleia laxa
Bulb; 12–30"; early spring; white,
blue, violet; sun to part shade; zones
5–9; *p. 65*

Trout Lily 'Pagoda'
Erythronium revolutum 'Pagoda'
Bulb; 6–14"; spring; yellow
with brown markings; part shade;
zones 4–9; *p. 106*

True Forget-Me-Not
Myosotis sylvatica
Perennial; 6–8"; spring; blue; part
shade or sun; zones 3–7; *p. 86*

Tuberous Begonia
Begonia × *tuberhybrida*
Bulb; 10–24"; late spring to fall;
edible flowers; various colors; part
shade; zones 8–10; *p. 143*

Tufted Evening Primrose
Oenothera caespitosa
Perennial; 4–8"; early summer;
white turning pink; fragrant; sun;
zones 4–7; *p. 53*

Tulip
Tulipa cvs.
Bulb; 18–30"; spring to early
summer; white to yellow, pink, red,
orange, lilac, or almost black; edible
flowers; sun to part shade, zones
3–8; *p. 172*
• 'Angelique': Peony-flowered;
  12–14"; pale pink flushed with
  dark pink; *p. 87*
• 'Balalaika': Single late; 16–22";
  bright red; *p. 96*
• 'Baronesse': Single late; 14–16";
  rose red with white margins and
  bases; *p. 56*
• 'Grand Style': Lily-flowered; 22";
  yellow with red flames; *p. 87*
• 'Mrs. John T. Scheepers': Single
  late; 22–24"; yellow; *p. 82*
• 'Red Emperor': Fosteriana hybrid;
  16"; scarlet; *pp. 90, 125*
• 'Renown': French single late; 25";
  deep reddish pink with paler
  edges; *p. 65*
• 'Spring Song': Single late; 18";
  bright red/w pink flush; *p. 150*
• 'White Triumphator': Lily-flowered;
  12–14"; midspring; white; *p. 111*

Tulipa kaufmanniana

Bulb; 8"; various colors; leaves
marked with purple; *p. 102*

Turtlehead
Chelone glabra
Perennial; 2–3'; summer; white with
red tinge; full sun or part shade;
zones 3–7; *p. 116*

Twisted-Leaf Yucca
Yucca rupicola
Evergreen perennial; 2'; fall; white to
cream; sun; zones 8–10; *p. 29*

U

Umbrella Plant
Cyperus alternifolius
Perennial; to 2–5'; summer to fall;
pale yellow brown; sun to part
shade, wet areas; zones 9–11;
pp. 219, 234

V

Variegated Bulbous Oat Grass
Arrhenatherum elatius bulbosum
'Variegatum'
Perennial; 12"; midsummer to fall;
silvery green; sun or part shade;
zones 5–8; *pp. 67, 139, 211*

Variegated Busy-Lizzy
Impatiens walleriana 'Variegata'
Perennial grown as an annual;
12–24"; summer to frost;
deep rose; leaves with white
variegations; light to deep shade;
Zone 10; *p. 147*

Variegated Forster's Plectranthus
Plectranthus forsteri 'Marginatus'
Evergreen perennial grown as an
annual; upright then trailing to 12";
leaves green with cream margins;
sun or light shade; Zone 10;
p. 186

Itea virginica 'Henry's Garnet'
Deciduous shrub; 3–4'; summer;
creamy white; fragrant; dark green
leaves turns brilliant reddish purple
in fall; part shade to full sun; zones
6–9; *p. 233*

Wake Robin
Trillium grandiflorum
Perennial; 16–24"; spring; white,
fading to pink; part to deep shade;
zones 4–7; *p. 181*

Wall Rock Cress
Arabis caucasica
Perennial; 8–15"; early spring;
white; sun; zones 4–7; *p. 210*

Wandering Jew
Tradescantia zebrina
Tender perennial; 6", trailing; pink
flowers year-round; leaves green
with silver and purple stripes;
sun or part shade; zones 9–10;
p. 146

Water Lily 'Charlene Strawn'
Nymphaea 'Charlene Strawn'
Aquatic perennial; 6–12' spread;
summer to fall; yellow; sun to part
shade; zones 3–11; *p. 219*

Weeping Cherry
Prunus subhirtella 'Pendula'
Deciduous tree; 20–40'; spring;
pink; graceful, weeping branches;
sun; zones 4–8; *p. 149*

Weeping Serbian Spruce
Picea omorika 'Pendula'
Evergreen tree; 50–60'; graceful
drooping branches; sun to part
shade; zones 4–7; *p. 213*

Welsh Poppy
Meconopsis cambrica
Perennial; 18"; spring to fall;
lemon yellow; part shade; zones

6–8; *p. 172*

Western Mugwort
Artemisia ludoviciana
Perennial; 2–4'; silvery gray leaves;
sun; zones 4–9; *pp. 83, 186*

White Snakeroot
*Ageratina altissima (Eupatorium
rugosum)*
Perennial; 3–5'; late summer to fall;
white; sun to part shade; zones 3–7;
p. 193

White Violet
Viola canadensis 'Alba'
Perennial; 10–12"; spring; white;
zones 3–8; *p. 181*

Wild Chicory
Cichorium intybus
Perennial; 3–4'; summer; clear
blue; edible flowers; sun; zones
4–8; *p. 75*

Wild Columbine
Aquilegia canadensis
Perennial; 2–3'; spring; red and
yellow; part shade or sun; zones
3–8; *p. 186*

Wild Ginger
Asarum canadense
Perennial; 4–8"; spring; reddish
brown, hidden under leaves; part to
full shade; zones 3–7; *p. 180*

Wingthorn Rose
Rosa sericea pteracantha
Deciduous shrub; 8'; spring; white;
ornamental red thorns on stems;
sun; zones 6–9; *p. 157*

Winter Aconite
Eranthis hyemalis
Bulb; 3–6"; late winter to early
spring; yellow; part shade or sun;
zones 3–7; *p. 178*

Winter Savory
Satureja montana
Perennial herb; 16"; summer to fall;
white to pale violet; edible flowers;

sun; zones 5–8; *p. 164*

Wishbone Flower
Torenia fournieri
Annual; 8–10"; summer; violet and
dark purple with yellow throats; part
shade; *p. 211*

Woodland Phlox (Wild Sweet
William)
Phlox divaricata
Perennial; 12"; spring; blue; part
to full shade; zones 4–9; *pp. 82,
101, 119*

Wood Sorrel 'Iron Cross'
Oxalis tetraphylla 'Iron Cross'
Perennial; 6–8"; summer; rose pink;
leaves has deep purple base; part to
full shade; zones 8–10; *p. 186*

Wormwood
Artemisia spp.
Perennial; 6–60"; silvery gray
leaves; sun; zones 3–9; *pp. 46, 115*
• 'Lambrook Silver' (*A. absinthium*
  'Lambrook Silver'): 30"; gray, finely
  cut leaves; *pp. 67, 173, 193*

Yarrow
Achillea spp.
Perennial; 2–4'; summer; white,
yellow, pink, red; sun; zones 3–10;
pp. 91, 106
• 'Moonshine' (*A. ageratum*
  'Moonshine'): 24"; yellow; *pp. 33,
  103, 106, 153*
• 'Paprika' (*A. millefolium* 'Paprika'):
  24"; orange red with yellow;
  pp. 152, 174

Yellow Archangel 'Herman's Pride'
Lamium galeobdolon 'Herman's
Pride'
Perennial; 9–15"; spreading;
spring; yellow; leaves with silver
markings and green veins; part to
deep shade; zones 4–8; *p. 189*

Amaranth
Chard
Coleus
Copperleaf
Dracaena 'Tricolor'
Golden Calla
Golden Hops
Golden Oregano
Golden Pearlwort
Golden Sawara Cypress
Heuchera
Hibiscus 'Red Shield'
Japanese Barberry
Japanese Blood Grass
Japanese Maple
Japanese Photinia
Juniper 'Depressa Aurea'
Kale
Leatherleaf Sedge
Leek
Licorice Plant 'Limelight'
Love-Lies-Bleeding
Mustard 'Red Giant'
New Zealand Flax
October Daphne
Oregano 'Herrenhausen'
Ornamental Kale
Penstemon 'Husker Red'
Polka-Dot Plant
Prince's Feather 'Golden Giant'
Purple Brussels Sprouts
Purple Fountain Grass
Purple-Leaved Wood Spurge
Purple Oxalis
Purple Perilla
Purple Smokebush
Purpleleaf Sand Cherry
Purple Wandering Jew
Red Orach
Red Sorrel
Sedum Silver and Gold
Sweet Potato Vine 'Blackie'
Tovara 'Painter's Palette'
Tradescantia 'Purple Heart'
Tricolor Corn
Violet Stem Taro
Wandering Jew
Yellow Foxtail Grass
Yellow Moneywort

metric conversions

To Convert From	Multiply By	To Get	To Convert From	Multiply By	To Get
Inches	25.4	Millimetres	Millimetres	0.0394	Inches
Inches	2.54	Centimetres	Centimetres	0.3937	Inches
Feet	30.48	Centimetres	Centimetres	0.0328	Feet
Feet	0.3048	Metres	Metres	3.2808	Feet
Yards	0.9144	Metres	Metres	1.0936	Yards
Square inches	6.4516	Square centimetres	Square centimetres	0.1550	Square inches
Square feet	0.0929	Square metres	Square metres	10.764	Square feet
Square yards	0.8361	Square metres	Square metres	1.1960	Square yards
Acres	0.4047	Hectares	Hectares	2.4711	Acres
Cubic inches	16.387	Cubic centimetres	Cubic centimetres	0.0610	Cubic inches
Cubic feet	0.0283	Cubic metres	Cubic metres	35.315	Cubic feet
Cubic feet	28.316	Litres	Litres	0.0353	Cubic feet
Cubic yards	0.7646	Cubic metres	Cubic metres	1.308	Cubic yards
Cubic yards	764.55	Litres	Litres	0.0013	Cubic yards

To convert from degrees Fahrenheit (F) to degrees
Celsius (C), first subtract 32, then multiply by $\frac{5}{9}$.

To convert from degrees Celsius to degrees
Fahrenheit, multiply by $\frac{9}{5}$, then add 32.